To argue Logically or with Heart

Mind and Belief

Dr. Saida Seddik

_____

"We can argue with our opponents using logic and we can certainly defend the truth with it, but we need more than logic to complete our philosophy and our faith."

G. K. Chesterton (1874-1936)

To my parents and my best support Seddik &
Keltoum.
To my sisters and brothers.
To my beloved kids & husband.
To my dearest friends who stand for me.
Saida Seddik

## Dedication

In you I believe!
I dedicate this work to you all after a long struggle searching everywhere for the truth that can lead us to understand the rapid and huge changes that occur in our societies and how to harness them for a better future. It is a choice for people to take to launch new system after the end of socialism then imperialism, the system that could cover his needs and goals and preserve his rights. It's time to make choices for a better future where human rights and justice are served for every human being.

This modest work is for people who are doing their best to make the right changes in human lives. This book is for the people who dream to free themselves from the unfortunate consequences of modernization, where individualism tears apart human relations, making meaningful interactions between people increasingly difficult. It's a call for people to come together, to honor and even celebrate differences, and to work together for human values: human rights, justice, equality and to spread peace, love, communication, and light up everyone's life.

There is always hope for people to come together -despite the many wars that rage around the world -whether "hot" wars with real weapons or cold one. or cold wars with ideas and competition—all attempting to control the world.

As a small elite possesses the bounties of Earth while the rest of the world population suffer from hunger, diseases, political corruption, and ignorance. This situation endangers lives and makes it hard for millions around the world to live peacefully. I call on everyone to get rid of prejudices and to work together to make love and peace reign with all of humanity firmly rooted at the center of our understanding. This, of course, means standing up for minorities' rights.

In people, I put my faith.

Philadelphia, Pennsylvania / August, 2016

# Table of Contents

## Preface

## PREFACE

This book represents the culmination of many years of research, meditation, reading, analyzing, and building a system of thinking all aimed to understanding the tremendous and rapid changes happening all around the globe since the mid 20th century until the 21th century. We need to find ways to make sense of these rapid changes—changes that seem to accelerate with the passing of every decade and now every year. There is a strong historical movement led by people in the whole world trying to shift the centers of power, so that more people are empowered to fulfill their natural potential.

Nevertheless the transfer of power won't happen smoothly; indeed, most likely the needed transformation will involve a great shock to the actual system _imperialism power led by US and Nato. This system is in critical condition collapsing worldly, in European countries, and USA the Mastermind of the system. Indeed the extremist wars launching everywhere in the middle east and Africa explains that the imperialism and neo-colonialism system is facing a critical collapse and is falling apart.

In fact as imperialism crumbles, many western capitalist and neocolonialist governments are collapsing economically, politically, and ideologically.

Many annalistic theorists, politicians, and economists are claiming that the imperialism system is in critical condition and is collapsing worldly. Indeed the extremist wars launching everywhere is considered as the only interface of imperialism to give itself a shot of survival with military invasion and mass media. Moreover these wars represent the ideological tactics used by powerful authoritarian corporations and empire governments to control the world. I consider these wars in the middle east and Africa as one of the interface that could explain the imperialism system collapse.

As imperialism crumbles, many western capitalist and neocolonialist governments are collapsing economically, politically, and ideologically. War is the only interface to keep the system's power and

*form of these invasions*

to impose its authority. The current wars *in* are a source of huge amounts of money to be derived from the sale of arms and exploitation of Vast natural wealth in the countries that are invaded.

Indeed military power and mass media is the interface to keep the big corporates and empire government in power. Nevertheless the future draws new democratic states that would give people the power for new mode of democracy with new conception of justice, human rights, equality, and prosperity.

This transfer of power from the elite class, big corporate and "empire" governments that control the world to the people who actually keep the economy turning would empower those all over the world who claim their rights. These changes will also benefit the environment by reducing the greed and exploitation of nature by corporations and "empire" governments.

All kind of theorems are set up to approach this tremendous changes, and futurism is one of these important theorems. The American Futurist Alvin

Toffler in his books has approached these changes states in his book Power-shift : "However, to make sense of today's great changes, to think strategically, we need more than bits, blips, and lists. We need to see how different changes relate to one another. Thus *Power-shift*, like its two predecessors, sets out a clear and comprehensive synthesis—an overarching image of the new civilization now spreading across the planet." 1

Toffler's "future shock" refers to the great impact these changes have, and will continue to have, on all aspects of life— including employment, the economy and, most especially, the ongoing cultural shift to globalization.

I believe this shift marks the end of power-dominant civilizations toward the beginning of new kind of civilization, where power is much more equitably distributed.

The ideas in this book result from yeas of research in philosophy, sociology, psychology, politics, economics, human rights, and religion. I have drawn on all of

---

1 Alvin Toffler, *Power-shift*, Bantam Books, 1991.

these sources in order to come up with a strong intellectual structure compelling enough to help bring about the needed changes.

I had to work hard looking at facts and to find ways to integrate the different views and perspectives of many researchers But I have not only looked "back" to what others before me have said or written; I also look forward to a brighter future.

Let go back for a little before we move forward, to Winston Churchill who once stated: "Empires of the future are empires of the mind."

Nevertheless, We need to ask here: What would limit authority and super power in absence of strong morality? Industrial civilization system has given way to a new information civilization; we now live in an age of mega transnational corporations, out-of-touch government bureaucrats, consolidated media-power, mass communication, slave-wage mass production, environmentally destructive mass distribution, and mass education that consistently fails our students.

These major changes will challenge many of the old ideas of democracy. Nevertheless, change is in the air. People around the world are waking up, making great and creative use of widespread information technology. However, change does not come easy; it's not one-step process. The transformation will demand hard decisions; the people will have to work hard to bring about the change needed to realize new democratic states governed by the people, for the people, and with the people. Finally with people working together and united, the dream for a better off world might come true.

Indeed, the "Arab Spring" inspired citizens in many other nations to take to the streets to free themselves from corporates authority, government tyranny, and dictatorship.

Let first face the realities: we know that our environment is in a critical state; climate change is a reality—a reality, we have to face *now*. As we read the news of increasing and more potent natural disasters around the world, we are witnessing an emergency call for all of us to act—individually and collectively.

The transformation won't happen without people becoming aware of the seriousness of the problem and then uniting to take action. As more people become aware of the social, political, judicial, and environmental inequities, we also hear in response, globally, louder calls for justice and protection of our human rights—most especially the right to a clean environment, with access to clean air, clean water, and clean food. We all have the right to live without disease, hunger, and war.

We can't live in peace if we don't change our attitude toward the environment. We need to get together to transform our societies, to stand firm against the toxic greed of corporations and the corrupt politicians they buy.

Environmental, social, economic, and political justice is the key, and without it we loose our rights to live safely, to explore our natural God-given capacities and gifts. The gift of life itself tops the list of human rights that need protection—regardless of race, ethnicity, sex, or religious beliefs.

This book takes a stand for all human rights: the right of expression, the right of respect, the right of trust and safety. Without exception, I stand here for all these rights, and I ask you to work with me despite whatever differences we might have. We need to stand together now to ensure a future where all these human rights are honored. Only communication between civilizations, between religions, between science and spirit, can make this possible. The bottom line: we need to cultivate mutual respect.

It is time to tackle climate change, time for clean air and clean water, time for healthy sources of food, time to ensure every individual and every family has shelter from the elements. Without these basics, we cannot hope to survive.

## **Human Rights and Modernity**

"We make a living with what we get, but we make a life with what we give."
Winston Churchill

In his serious and objective approach to human rights and modernity, Sven Lindquist warns the contemporary consciousness in a very specific terms regarding the extent of the shadow of genocide in modernity, he states : "You already know enough. So do I. It is not knowledge we lack. What is missing is the courage to understand what we know and to draw conclusions'.

If we are to follow Lindquist we need an interpretation of history that looks at the past from an array of geographical and historical points of view. A more comprehensive vision of modern history and of the crisis of modernity will provide us with an all-encompassing landscape in which human rights need to be thought. Having as a background this vast landscape of the disasters of modernity, the Universal Declaration can be seen as a response to all modern crimes in which widespread massacres of civilians were involved.

The genocides and crimes against humanity committed during the First and Second World War should all be taken into account, as well as the genocides that occurred once the Universal Declaration was proclaimed. And looking at the entire history of modernity, the Conquest of

America and the colonization of the Third World should also be adopted as part of the panorama of absolute cruelty that the moral fiber of the Declaration opposes.

We citizens of the world at the dawn of the Twentieth First century should understand ours as a Post-Conquest human rights culture. Perhaps in this way, the universal appeal of the Declaration would come as a result not only of the world constituency of states that have signed its text, but also from the ecumenical jurisdiction of the victims of modernity, from which the Universal Declaration seeks inspiration and breath in the times of globalization and neocolonialism.2

Human rights as a product of modernity are hugely successful in terms of number of treaties and ratifications, activities of international human rights bodies, expansion into new areas such as relations between private actors, and real progress achieved in areas such as the abolition of the death penalty. At the same time, several contemporary

---

2- Jose-Manuel Barreto , Human Rights and the Crisis of Modernity, Critical legal thinking, October 2009.

developments may, in the long term, erode the concept of human rights as developed since the Age of Enlightenment and undermine support for it. Three challenges are in the foreground:

(1) the decline of state power, in particular the phenomenon of fragile states and the negative impact of weak state institutions on human rights such as the prohibition of torture;

(2) the utilitarian challenge to the validity of core human rights guarantees, particularly in the context of the war on terror; and (3) the loss of empathy as a precondition for recognizing the rights of others even if they are our enemies. 3

Though the Human Rights declaration is basically intended to be universally implemented, it has been politically manipulated by the powers of the North as a means of exercising domination over the Third World countries. After the dismemberment of the Soviet Union, the United States of America became the sole

---

3- Walter Kaliin, Late modernity: Human rights under pressure?, Punishment & Society, October 2013; vol. 15, p. 397-411.

political power. Liberalism and Capitalism became, consequently, the global principles of the "New" world order marking the "end of history" according to Fukuyama.

In the other hand and according to Samuel Huntington's theory of "The Clash of Civilizations" (the American quarterly *Foreign Affair*, summer 1993) the principal conflict of global politics would occur between nations that belongs to different civilizations.

Huntington identified seven of these nation-civilizations, among which is Islam, alongside the Western civilization. The question is not whether this view is valid or not; more important is the reference made to global conflict, a reference that points to the dilemma Third World countries have with regard to Human Rights.

For the majority of the people in these countries, who suffered and still suffer the consequences of the imperial and colonial exploitation of their resources, the Human Rights Declaration is understood as a Western product aiming at protecting the welfare of the Western citizens at the expense of the welfare of the non-Western nations.

This understanding is supported by the socio-cultural level maintained in these societies, a cultural level which has not yet reached the cultural standard of modernity and modern values. Moreover, cultural diversity which is used by military or semi-military governments of the Third World to justify their totalitarian political systems, is also used to justify the difficulties of the implementation of Human Rights. 4

In an interesting article titled Human Rights and the Crisis of Modernity, Jose-Manuel Barreto exposed the horrors of the Second World War and, in particular, the 'real hell' of Auschwitz', which are usually seen as the background from which the Universal Declaration of Human Rights emerged. For Rorty, we

---

4- Nasr Abu-Zayd, The Concept of Human Rights, the Process of Modernization and the Politics of Western Domination, international Politics and Society, 4/1998.

live in a Post-Holocaust human rights culture. It was in this spirit that the 60th anniversary of the Declaration was commemorated last year.

Such a contextualization of international human rights law is sustained by a certain interpretation of the crisis of modernity. Critical Theory and Postmodern philosophy -from Adorno and Habermas, to Derrida, Lyotard and Agamben- share the assumption that 'Auschwitz' occupies the place of the founding event of our times. Thus, the Holocaust has been adopted by the European intelligentsia and the dominant historical consciousness as the event that incarnates the crisis of the modern age. The killing of more than six million people in the Nazi extermination camps meant that modern culture produced the opposite it sought and, as a result, civilization collapsed.5

When speaking about modernity, it's always referred to the industrial period when the human civilization reached its ultimate progress in western. In the other

---

5- Jose-Manuel Barreto , Human Rights and the Crisis of Modernity, Critical legal thinking, October 2009.

hand for the eastern civilization, it is very appropriate to speak about the kind of "modernity" Islam brought to the world in the seventh century to explain how this modernity was carried out and developed by Muslims till the twelfth century.

Nowadays, Muslims, however, are very reluctant to accept contemporary "modernity" on the grounds that most of its values contradict Islamic values, or that they rather stem from human legislation while Islamic values are originated in divine revelation. The problem here is not religious or theological but it is rather a socio-cultural and political problem.

As the concept of modernity is connected with the industrial evolution in western civilization. Nevertheless , this concept was introduced to Muslim countries through colonization with the use of military power. For that, huge changes have occurred in economy mode of production, social values, and political institutions. As modernity concept was imposed by force to traditional Muslim societies, the assimilation of this concept was always, and still is, perplexed: It is that of the colonizer and the master, the enemy and the teacher. Modern Muslim thinkers are, unlike their ancestors, torn off between hate and admiration, enmity and love. In this context, modernity is desired because it is practical, but rejected because it represents threat to traditional identity.

As matter of fact, the image of the West as projected in literature and perceived by the elite constitutes an essential element in studying the problems that keep the distance and maintain the difference. All the political regimes in the Muslim world, on the other hand, seem to enjoy a mutilated modernity, a modernity without rationality. 6

Even with the case of Turkey, the only Muslim country ever to claim to be a secular state, Modernity is under military censorship. The absence of the civic society institutions, which is the only insurance for its continuity, is a very remarkable symptom of the mutilated modernity. In this copy of modernity, individualism is always considered as

---

6- Fatima Mernissi: Islam and Democracy, translation by Mary Jo Lakeland, 1992).

threat to the community's solidarity, although it is emphasized in the original essential texts of Islam.7

Theoretically human rights are absolutely universal as model, principle, and ideal, but in reality things are different as political practice in most western countries has not yet reached that level of universality. In the other hand Islam as a religion is also ideal, universal, and also very human, but the socio-cultural and political situation of most Muslim countries does not allow the original message of Islam to be decoded. The world needs to change in order to reach the high level of the model principles of humanity. A cultural network of intellectuals should carry the responsibility of creating humanitarian values worldly likewise : equality, justice and freedom between nations and cultures.

## Democracy and Egalitarianism

7- Nasr Abu-Zayd, The Concept of Human Rights, the Process of Modernization and the Politics of Western Domination, international Politics and Society, 4/1998.

same time hold that all people should to be treated as equals—that all possess equal fundamental worth and dignity. In this sense, a non-egalitarian would be one who believes that people born into a higher social caste, or a favored race or ethnicity, or with an above-average stock of traits deemed desirable, ought somehow to count for more than others when evaluating moral actions.12

In political and economic thought, Marxism urges eliminating inequalities associated with capitalist market economies. Interpreting Karl Marx as an egalitarian normative theorist can be a tricky undertaking. He tended to eschew explicit normative theorizing on moral principles and regarded assertions of moral principles as so much ideological dust thrust in the eyes of the workers by defenders of capitalism. Marx does, of course, have an elaborate empirical theory of the evolution of moral principles corresponding to changes in the economic mode of production.

---

12 *Stanford Encyclopedia of Philosophy*, "Egalitarianism," August, 2002.

Human rights established by the United Nations charter apply to all human beings—regardless of nationality, place of residence, sex, national or ethnic origin, skin color, religion, language, or any other status. Everyone, without discrimination, is equally entitled to human rights—rights are interrelated, interdependent, and indivisible.

We all came into this world powerless, we live for a limited time, and we all have right to live until our natural end. Fifteen centuries ago, and the second Islamic caliph declared frankly and clearly: "How come you enslave the people while they were born free?" (Quoted by Omar Bin Al Khattab).

In addition to filling a spiritual gap, Islam brought about a previously unknown degree of egalitarianism. From a profound fusion of transcendental, spiritual wisdom with a strong sense of community sprang a society whose major concern focused on equity and equality before the law.

As social animals, living with others is a necessity for humans. In his *Politics* Aristotle stated: "Man is by nature a social animal; an individual who is unsocial naturally and not accidentally is either beneath our notice or more than human. Society is something that precedes the individual.

Anyone who either cannot lead the common life or is so self-sufficient as not to need to, and therefore does not partake of society, is either a beast or a god."

Despite the capacity to consider others' minds—to empathize with others' needs, and to transform empathy into care and generosity—we fail to employ these abilities readily, easily, or equally. We engage in acts of loyalty, moral concern, and cooperation primarily toward our inner circles; but we often do so at the expense of people outside those circles.

The hormone oxytocin, long considered to play a key role in forming social bonds, has been shown to facilitate affiliation toward one's own in-group; but it can also increase defensive aggression toward one's out-group. Other research suggests that this self-sacrificial *intragroup* love co-evolved with *intergroup* war, and that societies who most value loyalty to each other tend to be those most likely to endorse violence toward out-groups.

Even our arguably most important social capacity—the ability to adopt the perspectives of others—can increase competition as much as it increases it, highlighting the emotions and desires of those we like, but also highlighting the selfish and unethical motives of people we dislike. Furthermore, for us to consider the minds of others in the first place requires that we feel motivated and possess the necessary cognitive resources. Because motivation and cognition are finite, so too is our capacity to be social.13

Because our social capacities are largely non-automatic, in-group focused, and finite, we can retire the strong version of Aristotle's statement. At the same time, the concept of humans as "social by nature" has lent credibility to numerous

---

13 http://www.aipmm.com: Paula Gray, "Human Are Social Animals," *Anthropology.*

significant ideas: that humans *need* other humans to survive, that humans tend to be perpetually *ready* for social interaction, and that studying specifically the social features of human functioning is profoundly important.14

At the most basic level, human beings are drawn together for reproduction. Like other animals, every human has the instinct to reproduce.

This instinctive need, and the means to do it, is not taught; it is innate. Humans gather together to survive and to prosper, thus the need to belong to a group is a part of each individual. And with this comes the desire to be needed by other members of the group.

A natural satisfaction and security comes from knowing that we are of use to others, that others value our contributions.15

This social grouping impacts social relations—including how to manage

---

[14] http://www.aipmm.com: Paula Gray, "Human Are Social Animals," *Anthropology*.

[15] Aaron Quinn Sartain & Alvin John North, *Understanding Human Behavior*, (1958) McGraw-Hill.

31

power, how to reign, and who to govern, and which laws to establish.

Egalitarianism could affect social life in different ways. Small-scale human societies reflect our tendency toward "group-ishness," Small groups helped to check social differences and competition, thereby allowing for larger and more resilient groups to form (Boehm 1993, 1997; Gavrilets, Duenez-Guzman, and Vose 2008; Wiessner 2002).

If egalitarianism is viewed as a "reverse dominance hierarchy," or a way to damp down hierarchical expression (Boehm 1993), then it is reasonable that relatively minor degrees of inequality have been found in some Upper Paleolithic/Late Pleistocene societies (Hayden 1995). Yet at the same time, these inequalities were never sustained for long periods, nor were they formally institutionalized.[16]

Blanton and Fargher (2008) argue, based on a sizable comparative sample, that

---

[16] Gary M. Feinman, "The Emergence of Social Complexity: Why More than Population Size Matters," academia.edu (2013).

collective or corporately integrated polities are found where leaders are more dependent on local populations for their economic support. By contrast, exclusionary rule tends to occur where leaders depend less on the local population (instead, depending, for example, on spot resources or the control of trade) and so feel less motivated or obliged to give the community its own voice.

In other words, in larger polities, the more rulers depend directly on their immediate sustaining/local population for their resource support, the more agency and voice that population is likely to assert; whereas the less rulers depend on their subjects, the more autocratic they tend to be. It seems significant that collaborative/consensual forms of decision making may forestall hierarchical development in smaller human groups that engage in high amounts of face-to-face contact (e.g., Johnson 1982), while greater degrees of collective action and democratic practices may require more rapid increments of administrative complexity in large-scale social formations (Blanton and Fargher 2008; Levin 2010).

Vertical complexity refers to hierarchical governance with a concentrated decision-making and centralized power. Horizontal complexity, on the other hand, emphasizes the differentiation of a population into various roles or subgroups.

Size has a great impact on a community: including overall population, maximal community size, and geographic extent. The various means by which social units and their members interconnect, reflects the nature and degree of interdependence and self-sufficiency.

Human egalitarianism (social cooperative networks that lack institutionalized inequalities beyond those based on age or sex) can be understood as a later Pleistocene social adaptation or innovation- {Boehm 1993; Wiessner 2002).

Although institutionalized social complexity (the emergence of societies marked by hierarchical leadership and

34

socio-economic inequalities) is post-Pleistocene, this discussion briefly delves back into earlier times because new research provides a somewhat different vantage on human cooperation from the later Paleolithic than the perspective that predominated a decade ago.

## U.N. Human Rights

When people speak about "human rights," sometimes they use the expression to refer to the rights listed in the Universal Declaration of Human Rights; a declaration signed by 48 countries in 1948 and has since been signed by many other countries.

At other times, the expression is used to refer to the aggregate of rights we recognize of all people—whether or not these match the Universal Declaration of Human Rights.

The Universal Declaration of Human Rights (UDHR) stands as a milestone in the history of human rights. Drafted by representatives with different legal and cultural backgrounds from all regions of the world, the Declaration was proclaimed by the United Nations General Assembly in Paris on 10 December 1948 (General Assembly resolution 217 A), as a common standard of achievements for all people and all nations. It sets out, for the first time, fundamental human rights to be universally protected.

Moving away from the Second World War, it is possible to see that the historical review of the brutalities of the 20th century is still very sparse, partially because interested parties do not want them to surface.

The case of the genocide of the Armenian people and the opposition of Turkish nationalism to its recognition is an example of the struggle for truth and historical awareness. The exploration of the history of infamy of the last century should also include incidents that happened after the proclamation of the Universal Declaration, among them the genocides of Cambodia, Rwanda and Bosnia. And, when China is rising as a world super-power, we should not turn away from the claims made by dissidents about the killing of around 80 million by the Maoists over the sixty years they have remained in government. Such events do not only constitute breaches to the Declaration, but they should also be part of the historical background that now gives sense and orientation to its letter.

Modernity was constituted not only by the hallmarks of the rise of modern civilization, as in the cases of the Renaissance, the Reformation, the Industrial Revolution and the Enlightenment. Modernity has also a 'destructive and genocidal side' because the Conquest of America and the colonization of the Third World are also essential to its formation. The crisis of modernity is not to be found only at its end but also at its very beginning, as modernity was born already in crisis. If this conclusion is reasonable, surely a fairer and more inclusive understanding of the Universal Declaration as a response to the crisis of modernity should lead us to frame the Declaration as a response to Conquest and colonialism too.[17]

Recognition of the inherent dignity and of the equal and inalienable rights of all members of the human family forms the

---

[17]- Jose-Manuel Barreto , Human Rights and the Crisis of Modernity, Critical legal thinking, October 2009.

foundation of freedom, justice, and peace in the world. However, disregard and contempt for human rights have still result in numerous barbarous acts that outrage the conscience of humankind. Nevertheless, because of the Declaration, we can envision a world in which humans enjoy freedom of speech and beliefs, and where freedom from fear and deprivation has been proclaimed as the highest aspiration of the common people.

For people not to feel compelled to rebel against tyranny and oppression, their human rights need to be protected by the rule of law. Promoting the development of friendly relations between nations must be a top priority. The United Nations charter reaffirmed people's faith in fundamental human rights, in the dignity and worth of the human person and in the equal rights of all men and women. The charter promotes social progress through freedom and better standards of life Signatory states of the charter, in co-operation with the United Nations, have pledged to respect and observe universal human rights and fundamental freedoms.

The full realization of this pledge requires common understanding of, and respect for, these rights and freedoms, as a top priority. Recognizing this, the general assembly proclaims this universal declaration of human right as a common standard for all peoples and all nations. Based on the declaration, every individual and every organ of society-must strive to promote these rights and freedoms, through education and progressive measures, nationally and internationally. Collectively, we all need to secure their universal and effective recognition and observance—both among the peoples of member states and the peoples of territories under their jurisdiction.18

Unfortunately, the rights written down in international charters remain dead letters in a world where the meanings of words change from one side to the other, one country to another, one ego to another, from your and me to the other!

People need to embody the essence of the charter by taking the time to understand what it says, and be open to insights that

---

18. UN, *The Universal Declaration of Human Rights.*

might arise when reading the articles of the charter. With this in mind, I will summarize below the main points of the charter.

They all call for right to life—yet millions of people die every day, without mercy, especially women and children. "The brave meaning of words," as philosopher Merleau-Ponty put it, leads us to wonder if "the right to live" has the same meaning under skies as different as those over Bangladesh and Sweden. Speaking of the "right to leisure" in a world forgotten by modernity—or, rather, plundered by modernity—can sound like an insult. If the "Universal Declaration of Human Rights" remains little more than a high-sounding legal document, that does not inspire people to enact its ideals, it would be little more than a sweet and fluffy daydream. Words alone will not stop the momentum of realpolitik. High-sounding declarations, no matter how well intended, risk becoming the new opiate of the masses.19

---

[19] Nadia Yassine, *Full Sails Ahead*, JSP Publishing, 2006, p. 103.

The Declaration enshrines the universal right to education. Yet, according to a study conducted in April, 2016 by the US Department of Education and the National Institute of Literacy, 32 million adults in the U.S. can't read.

That's 14 percent of the population. Twenty-one percent of adults in the U.S. read below a fifth grade level, and 19 percent of high school graduates can't read.

In 2003, 14 percent of American adults demonstrated a "below basic" literacy level, and 29 percent exhibited a "basic" reading level. According to the department of Justice, "The link between academic failure and delinquency, violence, and crime is welded to reading failure."

Moreover, 85 percent of all juveniles who interface with the juvenile court system are functionally illiterate, and more than 70 percent of inmates in U.S. prisons cannot read above a fourth-grade level.[20]

---

[20] "The U.S. Illiteracy Rate hasn't changed In 10 Years," *Huffington Post*, 2014.

To be fully literate in today's complex society, a person must be able to read, write, do math, and use a computer. Without these skills, fluid navigation through society and upward social movement are challenging to say the least.

Worldwide, 775 million adults—approximately 12 percent of the world's population—are considered functionally illiterate, with only basic or below-basic literacy levels in their native languages. Without the ability to effectively use the written and digital information in the world around them, these individuals are unable to help themselves, their families, and those around them.[21]

With these statistics in mind, let us now review the key points of the Universal Declaration of Human Rights:

\*\*\*\*\*\*\*\*\*\*\*\*\*\*\*\*\*\*\*\*\*\*\*\*\*

**Article 1.** All human beings are born free and equal in dignity and with rights. They are endowed with reason and conscience

---

[21] Literacy Partners Inc., *Literacy Facts*, February, 2016.

and should act toward one another in a spirit of brotherhood and sisterhood.

**Article 2.** Everyone is entitled to all the rights and freedoms set forth in this Declaration, without distinction of any kind, such as race, color, sex, language, religion, political or other opinion, national or social origin, property, birth, or other status.

Furthermore, no distinction shall be made on the basis of the political, jurisdictional or international status of the country or territory to which a person belongs, whether it is independent, non-self-governing or under any other limitation of sovereignty.

**Article 3.** Everyone has the right to life, liberty, and security of person.

**Article 4.** No one shall be held in slavery or servitude; slavery and the slave trade shall be prohibited in all their forms.

**Article 5.** No one shall be subjected to torture or to cruel, inhuman or degrading treatment or punishment.

**Article 6**. Everyone has the right to recognition everywhere as a person before the law.

**Article 7**. All are equal before the law and are entitled without any discrimination to equal protection of the law. All are entitled to equal protection against any discrimination in violation of this Declaration and against any incitement to such discrimination.

Article 8. Everyone has the right to an effective remedy by the competent national tribunals for acts violating the fundamental rights granted him by the constitution or by law.

Article 9. No one shall be subjected to arbitrary arrest, detention, or exile.

Article 10. Everyone is entitled in full equality to a fair and public hearing by an independent and impartial tribunal, in the determination of his rights and obligations and of any criminal charge against him.

Article 11. (1) Everyone charged with a penal offense has the right to be presumed innocent until proved guilty according to law in a public trial at which he has had all the guarantees necessary for his defense.

(2) No one shall be held guilty of any penal offense on account of any act or omission, which did not constitute a penal offense, under national or international law, at the time when it was committed. Nor shall a heavier penalty be imposed than the one that was applicable at the time the penal offense was committed.

**Article 12.** No one shall be subjected to arbitrary interference with his privacy, family, home or correspondence, or to attacks upon his honor and reputation. Everyone has the right to the protection of the law against such interference or attacks.

**Article 13.**

Everyone has the right to freedom of movement and residence within the borders of each state.

Everyone has the right to leave any country, including his own, and to return to his country.

This right may not be invoked in the case of prosecutions genuinely arising from non-political crimes or from acts contrary to the purposes and principles of the United Nations.

**Article 14.**

Everyone has the right to seek and to enjoy in other countries asylum from persecution.

**Article 15.**

1) Everyone has the right to a nationality.

2) No one shall be arbitrarily deprived of his nationality nor denied the right to change his nationality.

**Article 16.**

  1) Men and women of full age, without any limitation due to race,

nationality, or religion, have the right to marry and to found a family. They are entitled to equal rights as to marriage, during marriage, and at its dissolution.

2) Marriage shall be entered into only with the free and full consent of the intending spouses.

3) The family is the natural and fundamental group unit of society and is entitled to protection by society and the State.

**Article 17.** Everyone has the right to own property alone as well as in association with others.

No one shall be arbitrarily deprived of his property.

**Article 18.** Everyone has the right to freedom of thought, conscience, and religion; this right includes freedom to change his [her] religion or belief, and freedom, either alone or in community with others and in public or private, to manifest his [her] religion or belief in teaching, practice, worship, and observance.**Article**

**19.** Everyone has the right to freedom of opinion and expression; this right includes freedom to hold opinions without interference and to seek, receive, and impart information and ideas through any media and regardless of frontiers.

## Article 20.

Everyone has the right to freedom of peaceful assembly and association.

No one may be compelled to belong to an association.

## Article 21.

1) Everyone has the right to take part in the government of his [her] country, directly or through freely chosen representatives.

2) Everyone has the right of equal access to public service in his country.

3) The will of the people shall be the basis of the authority of government; this shall be expressed in periodic and genuine elections, which shall be by

universal and equal suffrage and shall be held by secret vote or by equivalent free voting procedures.

**Article 22.** Everyone, as a member of society, has the right to social security and is entitled to realization, through national effort and international co-operation and in accordance with the organization and resources of each State, of the economic, social and cultural rights indispensable for his [her] dignity and the free development of his [her] personality.

**Article 23.**

1) Everyone has the right to work, to free choice of employment, to just and favorable conditions of work, and to protection against unemployment.

2) Everyone, without any discrimination, has the right to equal pay for equal work. (3) Everyone who works has the right to just and favorable remuneration ensuring for himself and his family an existence worthy of human dignity, and

supplemented, if necessary, by other means of social protection.

4) Everyone has the right to form and to join trade unions for the protection of his interests.

(2)Motherhood and childhood are entitled to special care and assistance. All children, whether born in or out of wedlock, shall enjoy the same social protection.

**Article 24**. Everyone has the right to rest and leisure, including reasonable limitation of working hours and periodic holidays with pay.

**Article 25.** (1) Everyone has the right to a standard of living adequate for the health and well-being of himself [herself] and of his [her] family, including food, clothing, housing, and medical care, and necessary social services, and the right to security in the event of unemployment, sickness, disability, widowhood, old age or other lack of livelihood in circumstances beyond his [her] control.

**Article 26.** (1) Everyone has the right to education. Education shall be free, at least in the elementary and fundamental stages. Elementary education shall be compulsory. Technical and professional education shall be made generally available and higher education shall be equally accessible to all on the basis of merit.

2) Education shall be directed to the full development of the human personality and to the strengthening of respect for human rights and fundamental freedoms. It shall promote understanding, tolerance, and friendship among all nations, racial or religious groups, and shall further the activities of the United Nations for the maintenance of peace.

) Parents have a prior right to choose the kind of education that shall be given to their children.

**Article 27.**

(1) Everyone has the right freely to participate in the cultural life of the community, to enjoy the arts and to share in scientific advancement and its benefits.

(2) Everyone has the right to the protection of the moral and material interests resulting from any scientific, literary, or artistic production of which he is the author.

**Article 28.** Everyone is entitled to a social and international order in which the rights and freedoms set forth in this Declaration can be fully realized.

**Article 29.** (1) Everyone has duties to the community in which alone the free and full development of his personality is possible.

(2) In the exercise of his [her] rights and freedoms, everyone shall be subject only to such limitations as are determined by law solely for the purpose of securing due recognition and respect for the rights and freedoms of others and of meeting the just requirements of morality, public order and the general welfare in a democratic society.

(3) These rights and freedoms may in no case be exercised contrary to the purposes and principles of the United Nations.

**Article 30.** Nothing in this Declaration may be interpreted as implying for any State, group, or person any right to engage in any activity or to perform any act aimed at the destruction of any of the rights and freedoms set forth herein. 22

\* \* \* \*\*\*\*\*\*\*\*\*\*\*\*\*\*\*\*\*\*\*\*\*\*\*\*\*\*\*\*\*\*\*\*\*\*\*\*\*\*\*\*\*\*\*

Imagine a world that truly honored and enacted these rights! That dream remains possible—but only if people of good conscience take responsibility for them, consistently and with integrity.

At the top of the list of human rights we find the right to *rights* themselves. Next the right freedom and dignity, followed by the right to life.

These basic human rights become meaningless in the context of major environmental and climate changes. If world leaders and their peoples do not acknowledge a similar set of environmental rights—*rights of nature*—then all human rights will be compromised and eventually negated. We need *climate justice*: the primordial right to benefit from clean air

---

22 UN, *The Universal Declaration of Human Rights.*

and water, without which life would be impossible.

Many countries, and several international human rights organizations, consider the right to life the chief human right. Nevertheless , many countries deny the right to life. For example, in 2016, Indonesia, Kuwait, Nigeria, and Vietnam have all resumed executions.

Although it is generally accepted that China executes more citizens per year than the world average, the actual number is unknown because executions are considered state secrets.

The United States remains the only country within the Americas that still uses the death penalty. Despite the increases in executions in certain countries, the global community has been turning toward the abolition of state-run executions.

Human rights should be guaranteed to every person on the planet. Yet many countries continue to severely restrict the human rights of their citizens. One glaring example: the recruitment and exploitation of child soldiers in several African countries.

At the time of writing, three ongoing conflicts in Africa were using child soldiers: in the Central African Republic, South Sudan, and Syria. UNICEF has estimated the number of child soldiers active in South Sudan, for example, to be around 9,000. Officials in the country have observed children younger than 15 years of age engaged in military training, wearing uniforms, and carrying weapon.23

## Islamic Law and Justice

The *sharia* (Islamic Law) was basically established to protect human rights and defend them regardless of person, religion, or beliefs, gender, or race. Sharia is not that primer of tortures presented in a certain simplistic thinking, typical of mass media. It is the quintessence of that egalitarian spirit and its expression in equitable social rules, I have been discussing. Encouraging the gradual abolition of slavery, the Prophet (peace be upon him) taught his disciples that "people are equal as the teeth of a comb." This principle of equality was intended to govern all the relations of Muslims. Far from being a penal code and a catalog of punishments, *sharia* establishes a contractual spirit hitherto unknown by humanity. The political domain is

---

[23] *Project World Impact*, Human Rights, 2016.

the first to be subject to this spirit inspired by the teaching of the Prophet (peace be upon him).24

Hodgson asserts that the fascination of Islam for peoples can be partly explained by the culture of equity and contractual justice that encompasses even the political domain. The sharia was highly egalitarian—we might well call it "contractualistic."

A wide range of relations were left to contracts between responsible individuals, including, in theory, the entire gamut of politics. In principle, no one was properly a ruler until he had been accepted in covenant by the representatives of the Muslim community. Even the marriage law, in which status played a relatively large role, reflected this egalitarian contractualism.25

Many traits of Islam that aid human rights are not unique to Islam; they also exist in other religions. If we confine ourselves to traits unique to Islam, we will not find very much. By obeying the recommendations of the Islamic

---

24 Nadia Yassine, *Full Sails Ahead*, JSP Publishing, 2006, p.156-157.

25 Hunke, Sigrid. *Le soleil d'Allah brille sur l'Occident*, A. Michel (Espaces Libres), Paris, (1963), p. 235-245.

Law the Arabs, armed missionaries, were clement and tolerant. Islamic Law is a judicious combination of a corpus of rights to be claimed and obligations intended specifically to guarantee those rights.

Nowadays, the innumerable rights recommended by *sharia* are evoked only secret in-camera sessions; in public, however, the media zoom in on its penalties, presenting Islamic Law as an irrational machine that unscrupulously crushes the human flesh.

A few years after the death of the Prophet (peace be upon him), Omar Ibn al Khattab (the second caliph) ordered not to cut the hand of a thief who came from a region where famine was prevalent.

Thanks to this flexibility, *Fuqua's* (doctors of jurisprudence) will comprehend that *sharia* is not a rigid practice but a set of regulations obeying rational standards, that *sharia* serves humanity rather than acting as a sentry that hunts down weakness, as some fixed

interpretations may lead one to think.26

---

[26] Nadia Yassine, *Full Sails Ahead*, JSP. Publishing, 2006, p.159-160.

The rules of Islamic Law always exist within the general context of education dispensed by the Prophet. That educating system had the mosque as its epicenter, the beating heart of the nascent Islamic society. It gave top priority to remembering God, and to celebrate the sermons and the gathering for Friday prayer, effective reminders of faith. 27

Many of the traits that underpin human rights and aid in their fulfillment, originally emerged out of religion, but they have become so absorbed into our culture that many people do not recognize their religious origins. For example, the notion of "the fraternity of all human beings," which played a major role in the French Revolution began as a religious notion: If we do not consider human beings to be the creations of a single God, how can we see them as brothers (and sisters)? For example, Islam (and other religions), offer effective aids to the fulfillment of human rights.

Here, I would like to provide a brief list of the kinds of elements that favor human rights:

*Islam underlines justice.* See for example these verses from the Holy Book *Quran's* chapters:

---

27 Ibid.

Al-Shura, 15; Al-Nisa, 3 and 135; Al-Ma'idah, 8; Al-An'am, 152; Al-Baqara, 282; Al-Ma'idah 95 and 106; Al-Talaq, 2; Al-Nisa, 58; Al-Nahl, 76 and 90.

*Islam repeatedly emphasizes compassion.* First, Islam stresses "God's compassion." The *Quran* teaches believers that God "has decreed mercy for Himself" (Al-An'am, 12 and 54).

In the most important Islamic phrase "In the name of God, the Compassionate, the Merciful," God's name is immediately followed by the qualities of compassion and mercy. God has been described in this way in at least 320 passages in the *Quran*. At the same time, Islamic life aims to acquire the moral attributes of God.

Hence, becoming compassionate is one of the important aims of Muslim spiritual life. It goes without saying that a compassionate human being will be diligent in respecting fellow human beings' rights.

In Islam, only excellence in piety can make one person better than another. Of course, even piety makes people more righteous only according to God's judgment; it does not give them any special rights. This fact can be interpreted as a kind of egalitarianism in terms of rights. Islam demands respect for contracts and does not tolerate any violation of pledges.

Islam never consents to anything more than reciprocal action. If someone unjustly mistreats another, the "victim" cannot retaliate with an injustice greater by even one iota. Moreover, Islamic teachings always consider forgiveness better than vengeance.

Islam underscores individual responsibility. Hence, it does not, under any circumstances, allow one person to be punished for another's crimes. In Islam, people can be punished only for their own actions. Islam strongly opposes terrorism. The prophet of Islam has said that no place exists in Islam for assassination.

Islam does not allow anyone to kill civilians. Any representations of violence one may find in the Quran and the Islamic tradition ought to be interpreted and understood in ways that conform to a human-rights-base interpretation of Islam.

Even if we could attain historical certainty that some form of violence was perpetrated fourteen centuries ago—and such certainty is highly improbable—Muslims and non-Muslims have the moral responsibility to work toward global peaceful coexistence, to mitigate suffering on an individual level, and to defend a form of Islam that is compatible with human rights. 28

*Islam is not a religion of dogma and absolute vision.* It's about individual people finding their place in social life.

Indeed, after settling in the city of al-Medinah, the prophet Muhammad's first action, was to constitute an *ummah* based on strong legislation that gave rights to every citizen regardless of religion or social status.

Nobody was forced to convert to the religion of the *Quran*; however, Muslims, pagans, and Jews, all belonging to one *ummah*, could not attack one another, and vowed to give one another protection.29

Islam, the religion of almost two billion people, now stands as the fastest growing religion in the world because of its positions on human rights and. To understand the rapid growth of this religion, we can refer to its profound concern for human rights. Indeed, of all the

28 Akbar Ganji, Press Association World Press Freedom, *Islam and Human Rights*, June 2015.

29 Karen Armstrong, *Islam*, Ibid, p.14.

major religions, Islam focuses most on human rights; it concentrates on human' justice regardless of faith, ethnicity, sex, or anything else.

The father of the prophets, Abraham, gave this religion its name: *Islam*. He is considered the source of the three pole religions: Judaism, Christianity, and Islam.

Abraham (peace be upon him), the father of prophets thought deeply about the creation and creator. As the model prophet seeking truth, Abraham questioned everything. In his religious journey, he spread the message of monotheism by rejecting his people's submission to false dogmas. When they rejected his preaching, he had to emigrate with his wife Sarah from Iraq to Palestine. Filled with struggles, obstacles, and tests, his religious journey guided him toward the right path and to the lights of the internal knowledge.

In the Quran, we read Abraham saying to his people: "Indeed, I have turned my face toward He who created the heavens and the earth, inclining toward truth, and I am not of those who associate others with Allah."30

## Islamic Law and Modernity

Modernity as an enlighten western philosophy and ideology necessarily implies two elements: rationalization and globalization. By rationalization it refers to the realm of reason and "objectivity". By globalization it means an increasing uniformity in the way of life of citizens and cultures around the world – people drinking Starbucks coffee in Piazza Navona in Rome, eating a Big Mac in Plaça Catalonia in Barcelona, or Chinese, Bolivians and Moroccans citizens wearing ties and checking e-mails on their new iPhones. The two components of modernity – rationality and globalization – are relevant when analyzing the constitutional struggles in the Middle East and the relations between Shari`a law and constitutionalism. Constitutions and constitutionalism are tools to implement legal and political rationality. [31]Constitution is reason; legal reason from the top of the legal-political pyramid. Max Weber analyzed how formal and substantive rationality affects both theocratic and secular law; the particular feature that distinguishes modern secular law

---

[30] (Surat Al-anaam), "Chapter Cattle," *Quran*
[31]- Antoni Abati Ninet, Modernity, Rationality and Constitutional Law in Muslim majority countries, The Danish Institute for Haman Rights, 2015.

is its formal and logical rationality.32 As Weber continues, the process of rationalization progressively affects religious norms and beliefs. Sacred law that was implanted in different legal fields is displaced from these objective legal fields by reason. 33

In his discussion of Islam, Weber stated that there was no single sphere of life in which secular law could have developed independently of the claims of sacred norms. 34 The status of sacred law in Islam is an ideal example of the way in which sacred law operates in a genuinely prophetically created scriptural religion.6As Weber pointed out, processes of rationalization also affected the sacred law in Islam. But the inadequacy of the formal rationality of juridical thought made it impossible to have systemic lawmaking that would bring about legal uniformity or consistency.7 Constitutions have their own empire; they do not concede superior rule, only coexistence. Therefore, the conflict between a

---

32- Weber, Max (1978): Economy and Society, University of California Press, Berkeley (Ca) p. 809.

33- Ibid, p. 815.

34- Weber, Max (1978): Economy and Society, University of California Press, Berkeley (Ca) p.818.

constitution and Shari`a law is often inevitable. It is a power conflict between different realms because a full separation between secular and religious spheres is not possible in many countries.

The impediment is due to legal unification and consistency in Islamic law, and the fact that the Quran itself contains quite a few rules of positive law does not help establishing different spheres. The clash between constitutions (rationalized and codified secular norm) and sacred law (dispersed and non-rationalized) is even stronger because of different factors. First, the founding of a constitutional doctrine has been supported by religious language to consecrate undisputed legitimacy.

Both what is defined as constitutional theology, as well as constitutions themselves, have been affected by the colonization/decolonization process. 35

The modern Islamic reformation movement, which started as early as the second half of the

---

[35]- Antoni Abati Ninet, The Danish Institute for Haman

Rights,2015.

19th century in Pakistan, India and Egypt, tried to revive and maintain the classical rational theology of the Mu'tazila as well as the philosophy of Ibn Sina (Avicenna), al-Farabi and Ibn Rushd (Averroès) and calling for concordance (or adjustment) between *sharia* law and democracy.

Jamal al-Din al-Afghani and Muhammad Abduh are examples of the rational revivalist movement. The twentieth century witnessed the development of this Islamic rationalism on a wide scale, in Indonesia, Iran, as well as in the Arab world. Nowadays, the discussion about the meaning of the *Qur'an*, the validity of tradition, Islam and the state, as well as democracy, human rights and women's rights, extends beyond the boundaries of traditional religious institutions to be present in most aspects of the new civil society all over the Muslim World.

This debate began to seize upon the ideal of consultative government as a way to argue for the basic compatibility between Islam and U.S. constitutionalism. An increasing number of Muslim-majority countries are inserting "sharia supremacy" clauses into their constitutions, making any legislation that contradicts the provisions of Islamic law unconstitutional. This trend is a continuation of one that began in 1979 in Pakistan with the passage of the "Hudood" Ordinance, and in Egypt with a 1980 amendment to the constitution stating that "the principles of the Islamic *sharia* are the chief source of legislation." More recently, the newly adopted Iraqi constitution included a clause stating that "no law can be passed that contradicts the undisputed laws of Islam."

Intensive research on *shūrā* since the 1970s did not result in an innovative approach to deliberative democracy. Generally, the debate remained confined to a retrospective discourse about Islamic jurisprudence, focusing on the same questions as centuries before: What is the meaning of *shūrā* and its derivatives? What is the scope and necessity of its application?

Is consultation obligatory for governance or only recommended? Are the results of the consultative process binding or nonbinding? Who are the councilors, and who should select or elect them? On which issues is consultation allowed?36

---

[36] Janis Esots, Philosophical City, *Encyclopedia of Islamic Political Thought*, (PUP, 2012, ed. G. Bowering et al.), Princeton.

When a concrete political system had to be identified with *shūrā*, both religious and secular authors either adopted a conventional Western model or defined Islamic systems only negatively—in contrast to autocracy or theocracy. As a result, theories of Islamic democracy have offered reformulations of Western perceptions in an Islamic idiom, rather than as a real alternative.

Notwithstanding the great spectrum of theories, four tendencies can be distinguished in the contemporary debate on *shūrā* and democracy. Representatives of the first tendency, radical Islamists such as Sayyid Qutb and his adherents, see the superiority of an Islamic system based on *sharia* and *shūrā*; democracy as well as political parties and the sovereign electorate are condemned as alien ideas, evil and contrary to Islamic belief.

The opposite view, held by 'Allal al-Fasi and Khalid Muhammad Khalid, among others, equates *shūrā* with a kind of original or authentic Arabic-Islamic democracy. A third view, held by the majority of pragmatic or moderate Islamists, embraces the rhetoric and politics of democratization, and adopts several aspects of the reformist discourse. Apart from consultation, consensus, and *ijtihād* (individual reasoning with particular reference to so-called public benefit), articulate crucial concepts of Islamic democracy.

Often considered the ultimate reference for Islamic law, *shūrā* should be practiced by rejecting all forms of capitalism. Based on *shūrā*, a radical Islamist critique of capitalism developed, attacking those Muslims who had accepted the dominant global economy and the power it represented. Many of these writers and activists drew on the works of earlier thinkers such as Sayid Qutb, the Palestinian Taqiuddin al-Nabhani (d.1977), or Ali Shariati (d.1977) in Iran, but they also developed their own vehement criticism of the inequality, injustice, and imbalance of world power they saw in the capitalist system.

Their ideas influenced thinkers and activists linked to al-Qaeda, notably the Palestinian 'Abdallah 'Azzam (d.1989), and the Egyptian Ayman al-Zawahiri, as well as by the radical Islamists Abu Bakar Ba'asyir in Indonesia, and Maulana Abdul Aziz in Pakistan. Their condemnation of the United States reflected a wider and vehement denunciation of all aspects of Western power, including the "world-devouring" greed of capitalism. As the attack on the New York World Trade Center in

2001 demonstrated, if that power could not be defeated, it could be symbolically and violently challenged.37

The latter part of the 20th century also witnessed efforts in Egypt, Palestine, and some North African countries to create alternatives to capitalism intended eventually to generate equal power based on Islamic foundations.

In Morocco, since the early 20th century [1920-1926] many have made calls to establish an Islamic state like that founded by Mohamed Abdelkarim Alkhattabi. He succeeded in founding an independent Islamic state with its own constitution, institutions, army, and monetary system. One may think about it as Spanish colonial resistance, but it was more than resistance. Nevertheless the horrible offensive military led by U.S., France, Spain got used chemical weapons pushed Mr. Alkhattabi to resign and be exiled to Reunion, a small island off the coast of Madagascar. The catastrophic war killed thousands of civilians but the people resign. This anti-colonialism resistance was successful in pushing away the Spanish colonialist. Many revolutionary

37 Janis Esots, Philosophical City, *Encyclopedia of Islamic Political Thought*, (PUP, 2012, ed. G. Bowering et al.), Princeton.

71

movements around the world were inspired by its resistance army tactics and developed guerrilla.

One result was the development of "Islamic economics," which attempts to create models of economic growth and efficiency that draw heavily on the established field of "positive economics" but tries to infuse it with values and preferences compatible with Islamic principles. As an alternative system, it suffers from a lack of practical application. Even those states that stress their Islamic identities run their national economies in conformity with the rules of the global market.

More visible and more successful has been the emergence of Islamic banking as a distinct financial sector in the global economy, tentatively at first and then, after about 1990, with increasing confidence and a growing market share.

The Islamic banks define themselves with reference to a strict but imaginative application of Islamic principles to financial practices. These involve not simply the avoidance of all interest-bearing transactions but also measures such as *mushāraka* (joint capital ventures) and *muḍāraba* (joint ventures

72

between capital and enterprise), which had long been sanctioned by Islamic jurisprudence as legitimate ways of using capital productively.

Although scarcely a challenge to capitalism as a system, the Islamic banks seek to put into practice, within the confines of successful financial institutions, principles that demonstrate that Islamic values are wholly compatible with the pursuit of profit. 38

Many Muslim political leaders were inspired by the European secular states founded on constitutional democracy. Nevertheless, these states were founded in opposition to absolute monarchs, especially in France, that ended up with the famous Diplomatic Revolution of 1756.

Some Muslim reformists were more moderate, while taking their inspiration from European democracy, they also aimed to keep the Islamic laws.

In his book *Islam, Secularism, and Liberal Democracy*, Nader Hashemi looks specifically at 17th century Europe and convincingly argues

---

[38] Janis Esots, Philosophical City, *Encyclopedia of Islamic Political Thought*, ed. G. Bowering, Princeton, 2012.

that secularism on the old continent did not develop in opposition to religion, but rather out of, and along the lines of, a religious-reformist agenda.

Hashemi argues that democratic reforms which implies the separation of religion from politics would be impossible, however the freedom as democratic value is spread in most Muslim governments. In the statistic outcome released by Freedom House, a respected non-governmental organization that monitors global democratic development, show that most population in Muslim nation which is 800 Millions is considered "free" or "partly free."

Indeed the establishment of democracy in Muslim countries requires the participation of Muslim intellectuals and religious-based parties who believes that Islamic law doesn't opposed democracy, modernity, or progress.

Moreover, in contemporary Iran, democratic leaders of the Green Party have successfully reconciled their understanding of Islam with secularism, human rights, democracy, and gender equality.39

---

[39] Nader Hashemi talks to Lewis Gropp, "Islam, Sharia Law and Democracy," Reset Doc, Philosophy and Religion, (March, 2011)

Nader Hashemi concluded by expressing a strong belief in Islamic democratization and secularization. The debate on the normative role of religion in government continues. This partly explains why there is so much political upheaval in Muslim societies today and why they are so vertiginous.40

A different conception of Islam and modernism was founded in theory and practice by a high-ranking Islamic scholar, Imam Yassine, founder and leader of the school and movement known as "Justice and Spirituality." His thorough-going theoretical project is considered an original approach to the modern Muslim societies. He wrote many books solving political, economical, religious issues, and discussed different opponent's visions.

One of his books, I read in Arabic, was translated from its original language French to English. The book is titled  as *Winning the Modern World for Islam.*,41 considered by the author as Muslim vision based on total

---

40. Nader Hashemi talks to Lewis Gropp, "Islam, Sharia Law and Democracy," Reset Doc, Philosophy and Religion, (March, 2011)

41 Abdessalam Yassine, *Winning the Modern World for Islam*. Translated from the French by Martin Jenni Justice and Spirituality Publishing, 2000.

submission to God. In this book the author approaches modern issues and democracy from an existentialism view connecting humanity to modernity values.

The original French version intend to sensualize modern generation about modernity challenges: neo-colonization, and imperialism that put their lives in endless struggle and complete demolition of moral and humanitarian values. It was a call for how to make Islam modern and accepted by European people especially the French one.

In the other hand, the English translation extends this powerful call to more readers in Western countries, as English is worldly read.

The translator Martin Jenni claims that the French title has a degree of shock value of inverting the secularist phrase "moderniser l'islam" ("modernizing Islam"), with no adequate English equivalent. As "Islamicizing" works no better in English than, for example, "Christianizing" or "Hinduizing," and "modernity," similarly, lacks clarity. He stated his opinion: "Translating a serious and important argument is not an appropriate occasion for coining novel and ambiguous phrases." (Martin Jenni, translator, 2000)

Nevertheless , the French "modernité" as used by Imam Yassine refers to  secularism values adopted since French revolution "laïcité" French style secularism – that is an ideology defining what it means to be French neo-colonialism.

More than a hundred years ago, modernism—as a secular philosophy—was condemned by both Roman Catholicism and Eastern Orthodoxy as a moral danger. Condemning the ideology of modernism extends to rejecting the secular values of the, "modern world."

The author argue that Islamic Laws and manners, rejected now in French society, don't oppose the secularism and modernity. In contrary these Islamic laws could be a positive solution to modernity and capitalism issues. Likewise the *zakah* (alms tax) considered as a tool for economic justice,  it's the foundation for the equitable distribution of wealth among members of a prospering society.

Moreover, the Islamic economic justice opposed the corporate-profit-that causes all kind of injustice in western societies. However the scholar Yassine argue that the western democracy may differ from Qur'ānic principle of consultative self–government (*shurah*), but its tools like honest election, ability to vote, free press, are very efficient in modern societies.

The Western suspicion that *sharia* would be less efficient than the current system of Western judicial law remains subject to debate. Nevertheless , in the absence of a complete and original model of Islamic law, it's hard to prejudge the Islamic judicial system.42

Many modern Muslim reformists claim that equality is the primary concern in the Islamic judicial system—with justice for all individuals as a fundamental human right. Indeed, any modern legal system in the Muslim world that seeks to draw upon *sharia* law will have to deal with the principle of equality for non-Muslims and justice for religious minorities. There is no avoiding these important ethical issues, as well as the status of women under *sharia* law.

*Sharia* does not presume that Islamic law "always" views non-Muslims as second-class citizens and "always" discriminates against religious minorities. That view suggests a certain essentialized and fossilized view of Islam; that it is (allegedly) forever struck in a pre-modern mindset and that it cannot evolve,

78

adapt, or reform itself due to its basic nature. Based on close study of the *Quran*, many important Muslim thinkers' totally reject this pre-judgment. They all claim that Islam doesn't need reform concerning the principle of equality and the rights of minorities, because Islam is already based on equality of rights. Some Western scholars also understand this, reminding me of the famous line from Lord Cromer, the British colonial administrator in Egypt, who quipped, "Islam reformed is Islam no longer." 43

The Egyptian thinker Abu Zayd, one of the most respected and influential Muslim reformists, explains that, contrary to widespread belief, within the Muslim world many reformist organizations exist, spreading the principles of liberalism, equality, democracy, and human rights. Unfortunately, however, for the most part, the West does not acknowledge this, and instead of contributing to strengthening these tendencies, it tends to emphasize Islam's negative aspects and, in particular, its links with terrorism.

According to Abu Zayd, the problem does not lie in Islam or in the *Quran*, but rather in

---

43 Nader Hashemi talks to Lewis Gropp, Islam, Sharia law and democracy, 03/2011, published by Reset-Doc.

the stubbornness that characterizes extremists in interpreting the Holy Book in a rigid and literal manner, without allowing for any kind of critical debate. Applying hermeneutics (interpretation) to the *Quran* would facilitate understanding it, quite possibly leading to a more current interpretation, opening the way to a modernization of the text without corrupting its inherent sacredness.44

## Imperialism facing Impasse

"There is no way to peace. Peace is the way."
—A. J. Muste

We always have the choice: Go to war or go for communication. War is not the only way to solve differences and disagreements. Indeed communication should aim to peace rather than fighting and pushing for wars to monopolize natural resources. We should be aware of the consequences of such decision, it's the destruction that harms lives and blocks the development of many countries. Wars go hand in hand with environmental destruction, which could be fatal for all human beings and nature itself.

---

44 From an interview published by Reset-DoC, June 2010.

Civilization, culture, and knowledge cannot be attained without true communication, dialogue, and mutual respect. Genuine human success cannot flourish without an atmosphere of justice, peace, and human cooperation—especially in politics and economics. Justice remains a fundamental principle in establishing global society. Much of humanity might agree on a new global social system that reduces injustice, is democratically accountable to all people, offers a decent standard of living for all, and operates in a sustainable relation to Earth's other living systems (e.g., see Korten 1999; Sahtouris 1996).

Determining whether this actually happens, and how such a just global society might be developed, looms large as a question for sociologists—and the rest of us. 2

This global social justice couldn't be applicable without a strong moral structure established upon justice, human rights, and equality before law. Much of humanity might agree on a new global social system that reduces injustice, is democratically accountable to all people, offers a decent standard of living for all, and operates in a sustainable relation to earth's other living systems (e.g., see Korten 1999; Sahtouris 1996).

In a pioneering book, *The Image of the Future* (1973), Fred Polak argued that we need a new generation of visionaries who can think clearly and deeply about sustainable social futures. The rights secured by justice are not subject to political bargaining or to the calculus of social interests. The only thing that permits us to acquiesce in an erroneous theory is the lack of a better one; analogously, an injustice is tolerable only when it is necessary to avoid an even greater injustice.

Being first virtues of human activities, truth and justice are uncompromising.45

I was particularly impressed while reading the chapter titled "Communication: A Genetic Need," in a book written by the Moroccan scholar Nadia Yassine where she referred to many western theorists approaching the neo-colonialism, globalization, and imperialism like Jean-Marie Guehenno and Dominique Wolton. Guehenno who is a former French diplomat,

45 - John Rawls, *A Theory of Justice*, Belknap Press, Harvard University Cambridge, MA, 1999, p. 3.

82

was named president and CEO of International Crisis Group in August 2014, succeeding Louise Arbour. He served as the United Nations' under-Secretary-General for Peacekeeping Operations from 2000 to August 2008. He is a non-resident senior fellow at the Brookings Institution. Before joining Crisis Group he was director of the Center for International Conflict Resolution at Columbia University's School of International and Public Affairs. He also served as associate director of the Arnold A. Saltzman Institute of War and Peace Studies at SIPA and directed the School's International Conflict Resolution specialization.

Guéhenno was elected Chairman of the Henri Dunant Centre for Humanitarian Dialogue (HD) board at the end of 2010. From March to July 2012, he temporarily stood down from the board to serve as Deputy Joint Special Envoy of the United Nations and the League of Arab States on Syria. He resumed his role as a Member and Chairman of the HD Centre Board in November 2012.46 Guéhenno, who

---

[46]- https://en.wikipedia.org/wiki/Jean-Marie_Gu%C3%A9henno

had dubbed our era "an imperial age," he describes imperialism as chilling age comparing it to the Roman empire.

He approached the modern imperialism societies taking in consideration tremendous changes done to nature and the political consequences of the use power that alienates people. With great sensitivity and remarkable talent he describes the imperialism in this paragraph : The imperial age is an age of mirrors: it's all reflection, a pale world threatened by both precariousness and tedium, a world that must navigate between the storm and flat calm, needing the instability without which no wind will rise, but fearing the unpredictable breaks that threaten unstable periods.

This same volatility of a world whose elements are entirely interlinked, and which anything can cause to teeter, lies at the heart of modern angst. 47

Indeed the imperialism has deeply affected our daily life and our way of thinking and living. The industrialism economical system is based on production and consummation.

---

47 Jean-Marie Guehenno, *La fin de la democracie* [*The End of Democracy*], Flammarion, 1995, p. 112.

The world in this ideology is divided in two poles the industrial neo-colonial countries that control the production and underdeveloped countries which are the markets and consummators.

Might globalization really be the emergence of a "new object, the world as such,"48 a world devoid of meaning that man's influence on his history used to give it? Might globalization correspond to "the outburst of common and specific problems for all mankind"?49

What is this Damocletian era, menacing in its precariousness, ready to disintegrate under the feet of the meager remains of man bereft of his human nature? We live, according to Edgar Morin, in "the complex world." Complexus means in this context "woven together."

Nevertheless, modern communication often seems caught in the center of the whirlwind called "globalization."

---

48 Nadia Yassine, *Full Sails Ahead*, JSP. Publishing, 2006, p. 67. From Jacques Levy, cited by Edgar Morin and Sami Nr in "Une polotique de civilization [a policy of civilization], Arlea, Paris, 1997.

49 Nadia Yassine, p.67, from Morin & Nair (1997), Foreword.

Historically, communication is a primordial means to interact with others, to trade, grow an economy, engage in politics, and create culture. According to Dominique Wolton's definition, communication belongs to the same reference system as democracy and modernity. Between these merely superficially homogenous aspects, Nevertheless , a profound imbalance is materializing whose pressure is gradually felt in the modern world.50

Justice reigns as the absolute priority for all social institutions, just as truth remains the priority for all systems of thought. We must reject or revise any theory, however elegant and economical, if it distorts or contradicts truth; likewise, laws and institutions, no matter how efficient and well arranged, must be reformed or abolished when unjust. 51

Rights secured by justice cannot be subject to political bargaining or to the calculus of social interests. The only thing that permits us to embrace an erroneous theory is the lack of a better one; analogously, an injustice is

---

50 Nadia Yassine, Full Sails Ahead, JSP.Publishing, 2006, p. 70.

51 John Rawls, *A Theory of Justice*, Belknap Press, Harvard University Cambridge, MA, 1999, p. 3.

tolerable only when it is necessary to avoid an even greater injustice. As priority virtues for all human activities, truth and justice cannot be compromised. 52

Communication should be applied without ethnic, religious, or gender discrimination, and without any form of racism—especially when minorities' rights might be compromised. Justice should be the first right and commandment for all humans.

Moroccan scholar Nadia Yassine (2006), argued that communication is a genetic need.

"Might globalization really be the emergence of a "new object, the world as such,"53 a world devoid of meaning that man's influence on his history used to give it? Might globalization correspond to "the outburst of common and specific problems for all mankind"?54

52 John Rawls, *A Theory of Justice*, Belknap Press, Harvard University Cambridge, MA, 1999, p. 4.

53 Nadia Yassine, *Full Sails Ahead*, JSP. Publishing, 2006, p. 67. From Jacques Levy, cited by Edgar Morin and Sami Nr in "Une politique de civilization [a policy of civilization], Arlea, Paris, 1997.

54 Nadia Yassine, p.67, from Morin & Nair (1997), Foreword.

I consider communication as the key in human successful relationship and a beneficial tool to achieve the best results in standing together to defend our causes. A current and urgent example can be heard in the loud calls for climate justice. It's not just a call for the right to survive, to confront hunger, to stop nuclear wars and genocide; it's a call from the human soul that shouldn't be ignored.

## Imperialism and Capitalism

The western civilization is based ideologically upon capitalism as mode of production and tool of managing wealth. As it's defined, capitalism is an economic system in which the private ownership of wealth (or capital) is structured toward the accumulation of more wealth (or surplus). Jan Aart Scholte defines capitalism, within the present global economy, by the following five processes.

First, capitalism is a structure of production in which economic activity is oriented first and foremost to the accumulation of surplus. In other words, capitalist producers (who might be individuals, private firms, publicly owned enterprises, or other collective actors, attempt to "amass ever-greater resources in excess of their survival needs"

Second, under capitalism, surpluses are invested in further production with the aim of acquiring additional surplus, which is then reinvested in still more production, in the hope of obtaining still more surplus, and so on.

Third, Capitalism offers "abundant opportunities to transfer surplus, especially from the weak to the powerful. 55

Fourth, many other problems and conflicts remain dormant, because poor peoples in the South are unaware that much of their country's "limited surplus value is being transferred to the North through the repayment of global debts"

Fifth, "today, the structural power of capitalism is such that most of the world's population regard surplus accumulation as a "natural" circumstance and can scarcely imagine, let alone pursue, an alternative mode of production"56 (Jan Aart Scholte, Globalization, 95-96)

---

[55]- Jan Aart Scholte, Globalization, p. 95.

[56]- Jan Aart Scholte, Globalization, p. 95-96.

Nevertheless the Second World War devastated the colonial empires of Western Europe, leaving the United States as the capitalist world's undisputed superpower. At the same time, that war demolished the colonial system, giving rise to a new form of imperialism: neo-colonialism. Along with this shift from colonialism to neo-colonialism, another shift occurred from intra-imperialist rivalry to intra-imperialist unity, as former colonial empires joined together under the leadership of the United States into one imperialist world system. I have labeled this "Trilateral Imperialism" (in reference to the Triad: the U.S., Western Europe, and Japan).57

This crisis pushed governments to implement Keynesian economic policies likewise the New Deal government of Franklin D. Roosevelt recovery from the WWII.58

Similar measures were adopted in capitalist Europe after the war, resuscitating the economy and creating welfare states that

---

57 Anthony Mustacich, *Imperialism, The Cold War, and the Contradictions of Decolonization*, Global Research, May 2013.

58 Keynesianism argued that capitalism, due to its inherent tendency toward under-consumption, required government intervention in the economy to stimulate aggregate consumption through government spending and progressive taxation.

limited the worst social consequences of capitalism, such as poverty, unemployment, and economic insecurity.

The United States adopted a comprehensive aid program to help rebuild Europe and Japan, investing some of its capital surplus into the devastated economies of the capitalist world. The Marshall Plan, as it was called, was no altruistic gesture stemming from America's noble spirit, but rather a way for American capital and products to penetrate European markets. In the end, the Marshall Plan pumped $13 billion into the reconstruction of Europe, reviving capitalism on a world scale.

Along with the Marshall Plan, the U.S. pressured Britain and France to dismantle their colonial empires so that the whole third world could be opened up to American capital. Although the decolonized countries were seemingly independent, U.S. policy makers believed that these countries' only purpose was to "provide raw materials, investment opportunities, markets and cheap labor" to "complement the industrial countries of the West".59

---

[59]- Chomsky Noam, "Deterring Democracy," (1992).

Thus, the primary threat to the U.S.-led order were "'nationalist regimes" that dared to use their national resources to attain the "immediate improvement of the low living standard of the masses".

The so-called "Cold War," then, was conceived to be a war for U.S. control over the third world . The Cold War is often misinterpreted as a global conflict between the United States and the Soviet Union, the two contending world powers, with the U.S. working to contain Soviet ambitions of world domination.

However, as declassified U.S. policy documents make clear, the primary threat posed by the Soviet Union was its willingness to supply military and economic support to third world regimes that were targets of U.S. aggression and subversion (NSC 68). The Soviet Union thus served to deter and restrain U.S. actions in the third world, which was unacceptable to U.S. imperial ambitions. Further, the Soviet system with its "autarkic command economy interfered with U.S. plans to construct a global system based on (relatively) free trade and investment, which, under the conditions of mid-century, was expected to be dominated by U.S.

corporations and highly beneficial to their interests, as indeed it was".60

To be sure, the Soviet Union betrayed the cause of socialism after the death of Stalin, becoming a social imperialist power in its own right.

Nevertheless , its imperial aims were limited to the region allotted to it under the Malta agreements and the threat it posed to the U.S. was its willingness to support nationalist third world regimes resistant to U.S. imperial demands. The United States and the Soviet Union did emerge as the two global superpowers after World War II. But even though the Soviet Union suffered horribly during the war, its subsequent efforts to preserve an empire ended in failure in 1990. And the postwar prosperity enjoyed by the United States certainly was not the consequence of its military victory. By the end of the 20th century, all the effort to establish the great empires had changed. Except for a few bits and pieces, the empires that had existed a century before (and many for long before that) were gone. Efforts to create new empires during the 20th century

---

60- Chomsky Noam, "Deterring Democracy," (1992).

— by the Germans, Italians, Japanese, and Soviets — all failed.61

Flows of trade, capital and people that a century ago were channeled within empires now generally take place on a more diversified basis.

As a consequence of this substantial change in the political organization of the world, there were important changes in its economic organization as well.62
Further, the Soviet system with its autocratic command economy interfered with U.S. plans to construct a global system based on (relatively) free trade and investment, which, under the conditions of mid-century, was expected to be dominated by U.S. corporations and highly beneficial to their interests, as indeed it was".63

---

61- Michael Mussa, Globalization and the End of Imperialism, Why has the 20th century been so unkind to imperialism? The Globist, March 2, 2001.

62- Michael Mussa, Globalization and the End of Imperialism, Why has the 20th century been so unkind to imperialism? The Globist, March 2, 2001.

63 Chomsky Noam, *Deterring Democracy* (1992)..

To be sure, the Soviet Union betrayed the cause of socialism after the death of Stalin, becoming a social imperialist power in its own right. Nevertheless , its imperial aims were limited to the region allotted to it under the Malta agreements and the threat it posed to the U.S. was its willingness to support nationalist Third World regimes resistant to U.S. imperial demands. The United States and the Soviet Union emerged as the two global superpowers after World War II. However, the Soviet Union' efforts to preserve an empire ended in failure in 1990. Despite a widely promoted myth, the postwar prosperity enjoyed by the United States did not result from its military victory. By the end of the 20th century, all efforts to establish the great empires had failed. Except for a few bits and pieces, the empires that had existed a century before (and many for long before that) were gone. Efforts to create new empires during the 20th century—by the Germans, Italians, Japanese, and Soviets—all miscarried.64

---

[64] Michael Mussa, "Globalization and the End of Imperialism, Why has the 20th century been so unkind to imperialism?" *The Globalist*, March 2, 2001.

The profound political changes that swept around the world after WWII went hand-in-hand with important economic changes, as well. Flows of trade, capital, and people that a century ago were channeled within empires now generally take place on a more diversified basis. 65

## Imperialism and Economical Crisis

The triumph of the United States and Western Europe over the Soviet system proved to most people the superiority of free markets and capitalism. Free-market euphoria swept the globe, giving birth to the new world order of neo-liberal capitalism. Thus the era of Keynesianism and welfare capitalism came to an abrupt end, once again transforming the imperialist landscape.

The neo-liberal empire of today did not result from one imperialist nation; instead, it is the empire of transnational corporations, based in the Triad, and

---

65 Michael Mussa, Ibid.

enforced through U.S. and NATO military force.

Neo-liberalism will not lead to the liberation or development of Third World nations; it will contribute, rather, only to their further underdevelopment and exploitation, as recent events in Iraq, Afghanistan and, most shamefully, Libya have proven.66

Today's global empire, dominated by transnational corporate interests, stands as the most destructive and dangerous empire ever confronted by the human race.

In the name of freedom, democracy, and economic prosperity, this "neo-empire" continues to pillage the Third World at an unprecedented rate, leading to devastating wars of terror and occupation. The failures of capitalism should be clear to everyone not on its payroll, and the options facing humanity today should be even more clear: socialism or barbarism.

---

66 Anthony Mustacich, "Imperialism, The Cold War, and the Contradictions of Decolonization," *Global Research*, May 2013.

The Iraq invasion, a huge mistake, lead to destruction of an ancient historical heritage, killing millions and causing tension in Middle East. The evils of war continue unabated—despite devastating consequences from Iraq, to Afghanistan, to Lebanon, to Sudan, to Libya, to Syria, to Yemen. The U.S. invasions caused terrible and tragic civil war and we must ask: for whose benefit were these horrible wars launched?

As a result of the excesses of global capitalism, the world faces severe crises—economic upheaval, political dysfunction and a growing deep distrust in modern democracy polities. Pragmatic values, neo-liberalist economics, and extremist thinking result in genocide, killing of civilians, massive emigration and refugees.

Imperialism, represented by U.S.A. and its allies, refuses to intervene to solve these crises caused by endless wars and invasions in Middle Eastern countries. Instead, U.S.-led forces get more involved in war—seemingly addicted to war, always on the lookout for the next opportunity . . . the last proposal involved invading in Libya and Tunisia in order to control oil production and to oversee the Islamic movements in North Africa. France also participates through NATO, with the U.S. military backing interventions in many African countries.

The repeated failures of these military interventions and invasions risk the stability of the imperialism system, taking it to the brink of complete economic collapse because of the trillions of dollars spent on the military.

Focusing on military force leads to neglect of education, health care, jobs for youth, and social security support for elders. The recent major global economic recession has led to more poverty and the diminishment of the middle class exhausted by having to pay more taxes.

And, of course, lack of employment leads to reduced consumption and weakened markets. All signs point toward the end of imperialism, neo-colonialism and the end of the era of super powers.

The European economic crisis (the "Eurozone" crisis) negatively impacted many countries and pushed some governments to enact stringent austerity policies, ruining economies and causing currency devaluation. The crisis was so extreme, it motivated millions of Europeans to take to the streets to stand for their rights, in solidarity with, and inspired by, the Arab spring revolutions. These protests call for real democratic governance, where the people lead and take decisions, and where nobody is marginalized.

The refugee and the Eurozone economic crises have changed the tide of events for the benefit of the people, without trying to get back to Soviet socialism or communism, nor to embracing U.S. imperialism and neo-liberalism. In attempts to escape the horrors of war, many Arabs have moved from the Middle East to Eurozone countries as to that could build a stronger powerbase to defeat imperialism.

Only the power of people can confront and change the new-imperialism that serves an ever-powerful and wealthy elite. While Syrian and Afghan refugees swarm into Europe, the whole world has to tackle and solve the crisis. The global community cannot ignore or neglect these unfortunate people.

The economic crises in Greece, Italy, and Spain also pushes people to migrate to more economically well-off countries in northern Europe. If these crises are not regarded as requiring a global response, then we may ask what function and role do the U.N. and other foundations, such as UNICEF, play?

## Imperialism and Environmental Crisis

In many countries in South America, people have stand firm to denounce tyranny, racism, minorities and women rights, and the harm done to the environment: air and water polluted by using toxic fuel.

Huge corporations monopolize the world economy, endangering peopled women rights, and the harm done to the environment. More recently, indigenous peoples have spoken out to stand for human rights against tyranny, racism, environmental justice, and war.

As more and more people increasingly realize, we live on a truly interconnected planet All of Earth's aspects—from biosphere, to soils and oceans, to atmosphere—form parts of one interconnected living system with important cybernetic features. Thus, environmental irresponsibility in one place, such as the excessive burning of fossil fuels in the United States or China, contributes to negative effects elsewhere, such as to global warming in Australia.67

The Earth faces a massive environmental crisis, with the potential to destroy the basic survival conditions for human societies (and those of many other species, too) within a century or two. Issues of ecological destruction—as well as broader issues of social inequality and injustice—gain prominence, not by the actions of corporate executives but by the actions of some 30,000 people's groups and movements around the globe. These include environmental groups, indigenous movements, labor movements, health-policy groups, feminist groups, anti-racist organizations,

---

67 Joe R. Feagin in *Agendas for the Twenty-First Century*, University of Florida, February 2001.

and anti-corporate groups (Klein 2000). Such groups agree on many critical environmental and political-economic goals.

Berta Cáceres, a hugely influential Honduran indigenous rights activist, was killed in her hometown of La Esperenza, Intibucá. Cáceres was awarded the Goldman Environmental Prize after she led a peaceful campaign to stop one of the world's largest dam builders from pursuing the Agua Zarca Dam, which would have cut off the ethnic Lenca people from water, food, and medicine.68

Lately, in Paris, a huge demonstration of thousands people gathered to claim climate justice, and to end nuclear wars. Besides the people many governments held also a summit in Paris, almost 200 countries from all over the world gathered to solve climate warming.

On December, 2015, the negotiators at the COP 21 UN climate summit came to a final decision on the text they had been negotiating for years, by signaling their assent to a thirty-two page document,

---

68 *Democracy Now*, TV show, March, 2016.

titled simply "The Paris Agreement. Although not a legally binding treaty, the document gives the world its second global climate accord, superseding the 1997 Kyoto Protocol, and replacing it with a global map for our climate future, agreed by all 196 nations.69

Climate change affects the lives of millions around the world, and as its effects grow, causing cycles of droughts and floods, food production will be hard hit, making many more millions go hungry. Wars will likely be fought over diminishing water reserves (many experts attribute the origin of the crisis and war in Syria to lack of access to clean water). Climate justice cannot be achieved without ending wars. And without an international plan for justice, the lives of millions of civilians have already been lost, their inalienable right to life violated. The dead also include millions of children.

The divestment movement seeks to stop investment in countries and corporations that continue to ignore climate change warnings.. Nevertheless , a major

---

69 John Foran, "The Climate Change Project," December 13, 2015.

divestment demonstration in Paris planned for during the COP was banned in Paris. Governments don't want the voices of the people interfering with the profits of big business (which pay for lobbyists and buy off politicians)—a major factor in runaway global warming. However, although the Paris demonstrations got blocked by the French government, the justice activist movement could not be stopped, and a major march took place in Washington, D.C., as one report stated: "On Monday, young people showed that they're building the kind of cross-movement alliances that we need to change what's politically possible in this country. This movement of movements is broad, diverse, and powerful! "In an epic demonstration of unity, one-thousand young people took to the streets of Washington, D.C. for justice on race, climate, and immigration. This mobilization brought together a truly unprecedented coalition: the movements for climate justice, for black lives, for prison and fossil fuel divestment, for immigrant justice, and beyond.

"Together, we share a vision for a new, better economy that works for all of us:

one that keeps fossil fuels in the ground; protects the lives of black, brown, poor, and immigrant communities; and reinvests in healthy jobs and renewable energy. This is a huge deal. It's not the usual suspects mobilizing together anymore."

We're approaching a turning point that will lead closer to justice across these various fronts—justice that doesn't require a prefix. Simply: *"Justice.* "Communities of color bear the brunt of the climate crisis, displacing many from their traditional homes and homelands. The protests and fights of all these movements interconnect. In order to win, we must build solidarity with integrated power. We need to use the momentum already created to keep building the needed power base. It won't be easy, but working and standing together, anything is possible.70 We have to stand with those suffering from the consequences of climate change and the disasters it causes, ruining the lives of untold millions.Racism in the United States has reached alarming proportions—evident in a seemingly

---

70 *The Activists,* Deirdre, Katie, Sara, and Yong Jung.

never-ending stream of murders by police of innocent black men and women. Twenty-first century racism, the "New Jim Crow," also reveals itself in the form of the so-called justice system and the "prison-industrial complex," which incarcerates and literally enslaves millions of black people, out of all proportion to their numbers in society.

Lynching of African Americans is no doubt one of the most shocking and deplorable legacies of the U.S.—as was the extermination and genocide of Native Americans. Along with growing racism, all kinds of phobias are rising to the surface. We see it in news reports. We see in its extreme ugliness on social media. We seem to no longer have any filters against hate and divisiveness. Slurs that seemed to have died out more than 40 years now show up with increasing frequency in social media—as if they were something to be proud of, as if it's all a macabre video game where points are awarded for depravity and offensiveness. (Ask Deedra, Rascism in America: not better, just different, January 06, 2016)

## Imperialism and the Future

To have a long term horizontal view for the future, as futurists do, then we need to pay attention and look back in history to learn how to solve crisis. As we chronologically scan through history, we can see how societies have evolved through major stages. Historians have identified three major ages: stone, bronze, and iron (dates for these are approximate).

Futurists Heidi and Alvin Toffler have identified a fourth major new wave, which we are living through today. They call it "the knowledge revolution era" that comes after the wealth revolution, but we didn't solve wealth era issues and we still incapable to move to the next phase of history. Imperialism system which is connected with wealth revolution is itself a problematic that create globalization, economical imbalance, injustice, racism, fascism, neo-colonialism, third world countries, neo-liberalism.

According to the Tofflers, while history is complex and contradictory, it can be seen to fit patterns, which the authors identified as three great advances or "waves." The first wave of transformation began about 10,000 years ago, when some prescient person, probably a woman, planted a seed and nurtured its growth. The age of agriculture began, and people started to move away from nomadic wandering and hunting, and began to cluster into villages—the birth of "civilized" culture.

The second wave came in the 18th century when muscle was replaced by machine—the birth of the Industrial Revolution, which gathered steam after America's Civil War. People left the peasant culture of farming and came to work in city factories. This "wave" crested during the Second World War—itself a clash of smokestack-industrial juggernauts, culminating in the explosion of the atomic bombs over Japan. Just as the industrial machine seemed at its most invincible, Nevertheless , intimations of a gathering third wave, based not on muscle or machine, but on mind came to the fore—the birth of the information or the knowledge age. While this shift is powerfully driven by information technology, worldwide social demands for greater freedom and individuation feed on information.

With the advent of this Third Wave, as information speeds around the globe at the speed of light, we become more and more aware of the staggering cost of the previous Second Wave, the industrial revolution—the prime cause of climate change and natural disasters.

Toffler treats technological advance as a virtual given and defines knowledge as the "fuel of technology." He never asks whether human inventions and intervention in nature should be proscribed.

## Imperialism and technology

A powerful force drives the world toward a converging commonality, and that force is technology. It has proletarianized communication, transport, and travel. It has made isolated places and impoverished peoples eager for modernity's allurements. Almost everyone everywhere wants all the things they have heard about, seen, or experienced via the new technologies.

The result is a new commercial reality—the emergence of global markets for standardized consumer products on a previously unimagined scale of magnitude. Corporations geared to this new reality benefit from enormous economies of scale in production, distribution, marketing, and management. By translating these benefits into reduced world prices, they can decimate competitors that still live in the disabling grip of old assumptions about how the world works. Which strategy is better is not a matter of opinion but of necessity. Worldwide communications carry everywhere the constant drumbeat of modern possibilities to lighten and enhance work, raise living standards, divert, and entertain. The same countries that ask the world to recognize and respect the individuality of their cultures insist on the wholesale transfer to them of modern goods, services, and technologies. Modernity is not just a wish but also a widespread practice among those who cling, with unyielding passion or religious fervor, to ancient attitudes and heritages. 71D

---

71-Theodore Levitt, The Globalization of Markets, Harvard Business Review, May 1983.

aniel J. Boorstin, author of the monumental trilogy The Americans, characterized our age as driven by "the Republic of Technology [whose] supreme law...is convergence, the tendency for everything to become more like everything else."

In business, this trend has pushed markets toward global commonality. Corporations sell standardized products in the same way everywhere—autos, steel, chemicals, petroleum, cement, agricultural commodities and equipment, industrial and commercial construction, banking and insurance services, computers, semiconductors, transport, electronic instruments, pharmaceuticals, and telecommunications, to mention some of the obvious.

Nor is the sweeping gale of globalization confined to these raw material or high-tech products, where the universal language of customers and users facilitates standardization. The transforming winds whipped up by the proletarianization of communication and travel enter every crevice of life.

Commercially, nothing confirms this as much as the success of McDonald's from the Champs Elysées to the Ginza, of Coca-Cola in Bahrain and Pepsi-Cola in Moscow, and of rock music, Greek salad, Hollywood movies, Revlon cosmetics, Sony televisions, and Levi jeans everywhere. "High-touch" products are as ubiquitous as high-tech.

Consider the cases of Coca-Cola and Pepsi-Cola, which are globally standardized products sold everywhere and welcomed by everyone. Both successfully cross multitudes of national, regional, and ethnic taste buds trained to a variety of deeply ingrained local preferences of taste, flavor, consistency, effervescence, and aftertaste. Everywhere both sell well. Cigarettes, too, especially American-made, make year-to-year global inroads on territories previously held in the firm grip of other, mostly local, blends. 72

---

72- Theodore Levitt, The Globalization of Markets, Harvard Business Review, May 1983.

By contrast, Jacques Ellul,73 often chided as a "technophobe," offered a very different analysis in *The Technological Society*. He discusses the extent to which technology tends to augment itself (as side effects and fallout set the stage for new techniques). Oblivious to its effects on the environment, technology continues to roll on in its "merry" amoral way (for example, nuclear energy resulted from research on nuclear bombs).

A culture is characterized by the facts it values and by its valuations, which are facts. More scientists are alive today than in the rest of history combined.

Toffler does not explain why or how the steam engine invented by Hero of Alexandria remained a toy, or why the conic sections of Apollonius were not applied for two thousand years, or that Archimedes smashed the machine he invented, or that Leonardo refused to allow production of his inventions.

---

73 - In the article: Confronting the Technological Society Samuel Matlack argue that Ellul's provocative essay was a summary and explication of the main arguments he had put forth in *La Technique*, which has since become his most widely known book, published sixty years ago in French (1954) and fifty years ago in English (1964) under the title The Technological Society. Its translator is John Wilkinson.

"Today such delays are almost unthinkable," Toffler assumes. But assumptions tend to leave us with a "tyranny of facts," with a past from which we cannot learn, a present in which we cannot intervene, and a future full of terror—more for some than for others.

Many of Toffler's practical proposals run directly counter to warnings from Ellul: "It is precisely the need to diagnose and cure this disease [future shock!] that is offered as both justification and demand for the creation of new human techniques." Part of Toffler's solution is a call for parental and neighborhood instruction—although the "parents" and "neighborhoods" he names happen to be near Santa Monica, California, where the RAND Corporation has its headquarters; in the research belt around Cambridge, Massachusetts; or in science cities such as Oak Ridge, Los Alamos, or Huntsville. Let the reformer beware! In the end, Toffler allows the burden of decision to rest with private imagination and "social future assemblies" without any tradition to focus their discussion or any language with which to pursue it.

## Imperialism and Terrorism

In November, 2016, I attended the Paris summit on climate change, where 200 leaders gathered to discuss the consequences of a warming climate. The event, under the direction of U.N. governments, also attracted many divestment organizations, eager to stop corporations profiting from climate change. Bizarrely, for a conference on the climate crisis, climate change did not top the official agenda.

Instead, the representative governments focused on the war against the "Islamic State in Syria and Iraq."

Nevertheless , they did not acknowledge the role Western governments—in particular the United States—played in arming the "terrorists" in the Middle East with sophisticated weapons, training, money. And now that they formed their own Islamic state the West wants to put them down—or, at least, they are trying to do so, and we hear everywhere in the media that ISIS is the evil that to exterminate.

According to Brian Fishman, a fellow at New America and an ISIS analyst who's writing a book about the group, he states: "it's important to remember that the Islamic State is a "hybrid group."

He argues that: "There are three dimensions in which ISIS has to be considered". First, "how is it doing in the core areas of control in Iraq and Syria?" Second, "how is it doing spreading to the *wilayats* [provinces] outside the core?" And third, "how is it doing as a global terrorist organization, committing attacks across the international system?"

"In Iraq and Syria, ISIS is on the defensive from a year ago, but when it comes to the *wilayats*, they're stronger" as Brian Fishman states. He also noted that the movement ISIS could expand in other Arabic countries like Libya, he reports that they have moved a number of people from Iraq and Syria to Libya," adding, "to the extent that it's happening that's striking. That's the kind of thing people always worried about with al Qaeda."74

---

74- Brian fishman, Why Airstrikes Won't Destroy the Islamic State, New America, 1/27/2016.

However, in Democracy Now TV show, Phillis Bennis declares, that airstrikes done by USA government is not legal as it's not approved by congress and the permission for military interventions in Arab countries is based only on the 2001 Bush permission to attack terrorism and since then all these interventions were done without any permission. Moreover she argues that the chaos caused in Libya is no treat to USA, and military response to terrorism is not the best solution and are at risk to failure. Indeed Obama has repeatedly stated: "We shouldn't use military to response to terrorism because it wouldn't work."75

In some western analysts' opinion ISIS could be evil, fascist, and radical, But why they claim so? May be because they moved from weakness to power, from moderate Islam to a radical version. Radical Islamicists realized that the interests or "concerns" of Western governments in the Middle East region, in Arab nations, has always been to secure access to the region's natural resources— by whatever means necessary, including,

---

75 Phyllis Bennis, TV show Democracy Now, 8/2/2016..

killing civilians, causing disasters, promoting sectarian conflict and political division. The last thing the Western governments want is settled democracy in these countries.

Western governments, in fact, do all they can to *prevent* stability, social justice, political improvement, and true democracy that would allow Middle Eastern people to choose their own governments. The West does nothing to protect, or even encourage, the civil rights of Arab citizens—to ensure education, health, jobs, and freedom of expression. Instead of being free to fulfill these rights, millions of Arabs people live under oppression, weakened by authorities, marginalized socially, economically, and politically. Given the depth and pervasiveness of this oppression, it should come as no surprise that people will rise up to assert their own dignity and independence. Western government support by all means the dictatorial governance in the third world countries, ramped up arms sales to them in order to cause more conflict and wars. U.S held military sales to the Saudi kingdom and other Gulf allies, and since 2010, the

Obama administration authorized a record of $60 billions in US military sales to Saudi Arabia. Since then, the administration concluded deals for nearly $47.8 billions in weapons sales – triple the $16 billions in sales under the George W Bush administration.76 This military power and weapons is used against people in Saudi, Yemen, Egypt, Syria, and elsewhere. This is not limited just in the way of vengeance as killing without respecting human rights.

The U.S.-led invasions of Arab countries causes more oppression that can lead only to more terrorist bombings and disasters. As a result of the invasions, Arab countries and their people have descended into chaos and disorder, under catastrophic oppressive governments. Arab youth seek real leaders for change— motivating millions of Arabs to call for *jihad*. This call was the result of seemingly endless Western oppression, invasions, and wars in the Middle East. Now *jihad* rests in the hands and control of the leaders of failed governments, for example, in Iraq, Libya, and Syria. Al-

76
https://pbs.twimg.com/media/CgclzNkVAAAfNid.png:large

Qaeda that always have been connected with *jihad* is viewed now as an old organization that never succeeded in establishing a state. In contrary ISIS has successfully declared the Islamic state in Iraq, could defeat its army. What ever your opinion is about ISIS, the fact is that ISIS is a strong state as military power, has its own government, banks, economical system based on oil business. May be the Arab Spring was the best circumstance for ISIS to emerge [2011] offering its support.

The west consider ISIS as the closest to absolute evil the world has known for a long time. Although its leaders claim to be Muslims and to worship Allah, it recruits from among atheists. Many of its fanatical followers practice no religion and have criminal records. ISIS attracts them because it gives them cover, helps them avoid detection, provides them with automatic weapons, bomb belts, and sophisticated explosives—enabling terrorists to engage in large-scale destruction of human life and property.77

---

77 Paul Johnson, "Absolute evil Absolute Folly," *Forbes*, December 28, 2015.

ISIS has the capacity to transform petty criminals into master criminals and then give them opportunities to demonstrate their new skills. The religious dimension to ISIS, although spurious, is essential to its success. As an ostensibly stalwart upholder of the Sunni branch of Islam, ISIS claims the mantle of orthodoxy and the right to murder non-Muslims of all kinds and infidels (Western Christian, Orthodox Christians, Jews, and so-called pagans) and to confiscate their possessions.78

Still this "rebranding" program was paradoxically assisted by the rise of the Islamic State, a group that split off from the Al-Qaeda organization, partly in disagreement over the image-softening exercise enjoined by Zawahiri.

Although the Islamic State attracted many defectors and gained territory at the expense of its former Nusra partners, its assiduously cultivated a reputation for extreme cruelty that made other "terrorist" groups look humane by comparison.

---

78 Paul Johnson, Ibid.

According to Daveed Gartenstein-Ross, a senior fellow with the foundation for Defense of Democracies, many Nusra members suspect that the Islamic State was created by the Americans "to discredit *jihad*."79

Many wars were going on since The invasion in Iraq (1991-1993) was just the start of a much larger plan by the U.S.-led West to dominate the region and its natural resources, especially oil. then the war went on without stop until they overthrew the president Saddam Husain.

Saddam Hussein's Ba'athist regime was not toppled by a local insurgency, but by an invasion from a vastly superior military force. The United States could at least have attempted to damp down the chaos that emerged after Hussein was deposed.

The emergence of ISIS in Iraq, despite the fact that the terrorist group is gradually

79 Andrew Cockburn, "The United States is Teaming up with Al Qaeda, Again," *Harper's*, January 2016.
80 Ian Millhiser, The Writers Of 'Star Wars: The Force Awakens' Understand Regime Change Better Than George W. Bush, Think Progress, Dec 21, 2015.

losing ground, is a testament to the limited ability of the U.S. to shape Iraq's destiny.80

The same thing applies to Afghanistan with Al-Qaida; Libya had the same fate. The nuclear war in Syria grows increasingly more complicated with the genocide and refugees crisis. It's a complete disaster.

The philosophy and ideology of empires over history is based on population control, invasion, and conquer of colonies. This could be done only through wars, conflict, oppression, and clash. The ideological purpose is the geo-political strategy and economic interest. Nowadays the powerful empires control the third world' governments and its population with military power, economical interest, and the globalization of intellectual and cultural values. In addition, wars are backed by the most sophisticated human sciences: Ethnography and Anthropology; the participation of anthropologists in the counter-insurgency and so-called "pacification" operations of Iraq and Afghanistan initially became a topic when it was noted by members of the American media in 2006.

Around 1970, anthropologists often told their colleagues to shun collaboration with the powerful in neocolonial planning and strategy. Instead, they were supposed to support "indigenous" peoples in their struggles, to help the latter achieve the modernization that the legacy of colonialism—a perfidious combination of an ideology of modernization and a strategy of exploitation—denied them. 81

Without disregard the extent of American power interests in the Middle East, the "Arab World" and the wider "Islamic World", this "strategic area" is no longer only an American prerogative. The war on terrorism seems to have amplified a battle that was always already under construction, intensifying the effects of those studies-government-corporate alliances that Said spoke of. (Edward Said 1997)

---

[81] Peter Pels, The Anthropology of Colonialism,

Amsterdam University, 1997.

Nevertheless ISIS' ideology and understanding of Islamic law doesn't comply with the change the Muslim nation worked hard, through Arab Spring, to settle democratic states emancipating human being from tyranny and oppression. ISIS is a new phenomenon [2011-2016] created by the escalation and military intervention in Iraq, Syria and in Libya. Recently the military intervention in Libya pushed the escalation to highest tension. No matter how strong ISIS could be it could never be taken as an effective element in solving this horrible war crisis. Civilian [kids, women, elder] have been killed and injured yet there is no peace proposals from great western power but more war and escalation. Many Islamic scholars claim that ISIS is the military independent resistance power against western military interventions while governments like Saudi and else have abandoned supporting resistance in Iraq, Syria, and Libya.

We can't get peace from war, we can't get democracy from disaster, and we can't get justice from oppression. Today, the whole region is in high tension, and to solve this geo-political crisis, to achieve justice at all levels, many governments have to come together in search of a better solution: ending the war, not re-launching it.

Did the West really try hard to create democracy in these Arab countries, or it was just political propaganda?

Behind this question I wonder how much trust we should place in governments that would allow the Earth to burn from climate change —or from the nuclear war they plan to launch when they manage to stir up intense Islamic phobia. All just an obscene pretext to declare marshal law or a "state of emergency," as happened in France after the Paris and Nice attacks?

## Imperialism and Mind Control
The national security structure needs to be infused with anthropology, a discipline invented to support war-fighting in the tribal zone. Cultural knowledge of the adversaries should be considered a national                          security priority...anthropological       knowledge contributed   to   the   expansion   and consolidation of British power during the

era of empire [Montgomery McFate, Joint Force Quarterly, 2006]

After colonialism ended, a new era of imperial domination was forming that is referred to as neocolonialism. Neocolonialism refers to the "imperial system of economic exploitation, in which the metropolitan center drains the resources of the periphery while at the same time encouraging it to consume its manufactured products in an unequal, unbalanced system of exchange" [Young, 2001, p.47.]

The concern in terms of neocolonialism is with contemporary power relations and global imbalances. It articulates how developing countries are manipulated and governed by remote control through the economic force of northern and economically advanced countries. It examines the inequities of poor countries, which must concede to the demands of the rich countries in the North, particularly in the form of trade and other economic factors. The theme of corruption explores the operations of the ruling elite in the home country and the consequences of their greed, duplicity, and corrupt practices on local suffering in terms of tribal wars, increased poverty, and human rights violations.

The concept of neocolonialism helped Joan in illuminating the attitude of local people toward corruption in their country, how the work of local activists is made more difficult by local authorities, the connect in local suffering and global inequity, and the levels of control the global North has over the economic futures of those in the global South.[82]

The philosophy and ideology of empires over history is based on population control, invasion, and conquer of colonies. This could be done only through wars, conflict, oppression, and clash. The ideological purpose is the geo-political strategy and economic interest. Nowadays the powerful empires control the third world' governments and its population with military power, economical interest, and the globalization of intellectual and cultural values. In addition, wars are backed by the most sophisticated human sciences: Ethnography and Anthropology; the participation of anthropologists in the

---

[82] Peter Pels, The Anthropology of Colonialism, Amsterdam University, 1997.

counter-insurgency and so-called "pacification" operations of Iraq and Afghanistan initially became a topic when it was noted by members of the American media in 2006.

Edward Said declared in a little-known text that the connection of military and scientific powers was an American peculiarity and that American Orientalism constituted a paradigmatic example:

"Similar scholars [the neo-orientalists] in the United States are known only as Middle East or Islamic experts; they belong to the class of experts, and their domain, insofar as they are concerned with modern societies in the Islamic world, can be regarded as the intellectual equivalent of crisis management. Much of their status derives from the notion that for the United States the Islamic world is a strategic area, with all sorts of possible [if not always actual] problems. During their many decades of administering Islamic colonies, both Britain and France naturally produced a class of colonial experts, but this class did not in turn produce an adjunct to it equivalent to the network of the Middle East studies- government-corporate

alliance that exists in the United States."
(Edward Said 1997).

Without disregard Without disregarding
the extent of American power interests in
the Middle East, the "Arab World" and
the wider "Islamic World", this "strategic
area" is no longer only an American
prerogative. The war on terrorism seems
to have amplified a battle that was always
already under construction, intensifying
the effects of those studies-government-
corporate alliances that Said spoke of.
(Edward Said 1997)

Around 1970, anthropologists often told
their colleagues to shun collaboration
with the powerful in neocolonial planning
and strategy. Instead, they were supposed
to support "indigenous" peoples in their
struggles, to help the latter achieve the
modernization that the legacy of
colonialism—a perfidious combination of

---

[83] Peter Pels, The Anthropology of Colonialism, Amsterdam

University, 1997.

an ideology of modernization and a strategy of exploitation—denied them. 83

In the other hand David McFate emphasize the cultural knowledge of the adversary; he points out that the more unconventional the adversary, and the further from Western cultural norms, the more we need to understand the society and underlying cultural dynamics. To defeat non-Western opponents who are transnational in scope, nonhierarchical in structure, clandestine in approach, and who operate outside the context of nation-states, we need to improve our capacity to understand foreign cultures [McFate, 2006]

In particular, numerous newspapers, magazines, and journals began to speak (with critical tones, or with tones of satisfaction for a supposed change of course by the American administration in the method of management of military operations) of the creation of a "Human Terrain System". This system was composed of "Human Terrain Teams" of anthropologists- American and otherwise - with the general task of rendering the counter-insurgency and the process of "pacification and reconstruction" effective in these two scenarios of war. The social scientists were requested to participate in operations of ethnographic intelligence. 84

It is up to the anthropologist to unravel the details of the human encounters that the soldiers experience on the battleground. The anthropologist must explain what a better cultural knowledge of the enemy could consist of and indicate how to use it in their interaction with the population: "Soldiers and Marines were unable to establish one-to-one relationships with Iraqis, which are key both to intelligence collection and winning hearts and minds" [McFate 2006: 44].

According to McFate, one of the key points in the lack of comprehension of the -local culture- is the soldiers' incapacity to use typical Iraqi gestural expressiveness and their tolerance for physical proximity. The soldiers could not understand the local complex symbology. In other words, McFate suggests an anthropology of misunderstandings that should help to overcome operational mistakes, and provides an example: some Marines shot

84- Nicola Pirugini, Anthropologists at War, 2008.

at homes that were flying black flags, which refer to Shiite presence, thinking that the black flags meant shoot here. Since the white flag in the culture of American war means surrender, the black flag would have been interpreted by the Marines not only as its opposite, but as the deliberate desire to be hit by enemy fire. [McFate, 2006, 48.]

In this article David Kilcullen defines himself as an expert of the cultural knowledge of a particular enemy, that is to say the Islamic Jihadists. He sustains that in order to try to understand and characterize jihad, the use of social and ethnographic models is essential. He says he wants to apply the models traditionally proposed by Middle Eastern anthropology to the jihad network, for a better comprehension of what he calls a global insurgency (2005: 603).

In David Kilcullen's words: "the jihad is a variant on a traditional Middle Eastern patronage network. It is an intricate, ramified web of dependency and, critically, the patterns of patronage and dependency are its central defining features, rather than the insurgent cells or their activities...fieldwork analysis indicates that jihadist military activity may actually be merely one of the shared activities that the network engages in, while the core is the patronage network." [David Kilcullen, 2005: 603]

To know a culture does not per se represent an aggressive act, far from it. But the empirical conditions under which knowledge-production takes place, and not least the finalities of the knowledge produced can easily transform the cognitive process into an act of aggression and into the production of an authoritarian form of knowledge and power. In a context of permanent war that brings the appetites of increasingly organic sciences and groups of political power closer and closer, one cannot avoid recognizing an ever more risky situation. The risk may not be that of an implosion of intelligence ethnography within the discipline. The real risk may lie elsewhere. The real risk may be a generalized exercise of ethnography subdued by strategic interests that, knowingly or not, will take control of the discipline, making obsolete the distance between ethnography and strategy of war: an ethnography applied in the name of a presumed modernization (before of the state, now of warfare). An ethnography applied to the causes of political interest and a presumed national security. 85

## **Conclusion**

Human being is always by its inner nature looking for causality to explain nature phenomena and historic events through the concepts: cause and effect. This human inner nature is based on logic conception or on faith. Indeed this human inner nature is what makes him special and different from other creatures. Moreover this human inner human nature is what makes human being ask questions and seek for causality in understanding physical and historic phenomena and look for the truth around him either by the use of logic or the faith and believes.

Beside being intellectual, human being is practical and for many millennia he has been tool-makers, yet in just a few decades we have developed social, economical and political system because of the high developed technology. Indeed

---

[85] Nicola Pirugini, Anthropologists at War, 2008.

human modern civilization has gone too far since industrial revolution—such as polluting industries, fossil-fuel consuming engines, and nuclear weapons—that may well threaten the survival of our species and of the living planet itself. It seems likely that the fate of our planet and its species will be decided within the next few generations by just one of its species—*ours*. As moral beings, we need to ask insistently: *What would alternatives to our self-destructive societies look like? And how do we get there?*

Much of humanity might agree on a new global social system that reduces injustice, is democratically accountable to all people, offers a decent standard of living for all, and operates in a sustainable relation to Earth's other living systems (e.g., see Korten 1999; Sahtouris 1996). Determining whether this is the case and how such a just global society might be developed are enormous questions that sociologists—and other citizens of the world—should be tackling.

In a pioneering book, *The Image of the Future* (1973), Fred Polak argued that we need a new generation of visionaries who can think clearly and deeply about sustainable social futures. Whether social scientist, intellectual, artist, leader, entrepreneurs, and the common citizens, we all must ask: *What is my vision of the future? And what am I going to do about it?* (p. 305)

While social science analysis can help us understand our ailing societal dreams and decide what dreams to accept or reject, such analysis is beneficial only if it frees us to decide on a better future.

Let me conclude by closely paraphrasing Polak (1973, p. 305): Human beings have the ability to dream better futures than we have yet succeeded in dreaming. We have the ability to create much better societies than we have yet succeeded in creating.

We conclude that tyranny (in all its forms: intellectual, political, or religious), and dictatorship (even masked under modernity and new democracy) do not respond to the human call for real democracy, where the people have the right to speak out freely, and have the capability to protect their rights.

In an earlier chapter, I outlined the U.N. charter on human rights. The real and urgent issue now is how to bring these rights to our lives, how to make real changes in our societies, our economies. How do we solve educational problems, and make education available to child? How do we stop the endless wars that destroy our lives? How do we stop destroying the natural environment and keep it clean and healthy for generations to come?

With these questions in mind: most of all don't let yourself be passive. Stand up for the cause of universal human rights and shout out, like the speaker and singer who declared: "I admit being a traitor. I'm a traitor to imperialism, neo-colonialism, murder and torture."

We all need to fight systematic racism, economic exploitation, and imperialism; we all need to fight for justice of all kinds —including, and most especially, *climate justice*, Don't let greedy corporations and the governments they buy destroy the bounties of the nature. We all need to do whatever it takes to stop them from polluting our water, air, and food.

Claim your rights to health, education, a secure, well-paying job, and your personal and national dignity. Take a united stand for justice, human rights, and freedom. Stay positive, work to change the whole world.

In the end, we will succeed in this truly "life-saving" mission only if we communicate our values in a civilized manner, instead of imposing them with oppression and war. Democracy is a right of choice not a system to impose.

## Bibliography

Abdessalam Yassine, *Winning the Modern World for Islam*, Translated from the French by Martin Jenni Justice and Spirituality Publishing, 2000.

Alvin Toffler, the Third wave, 1984.

Akbar Ganji, Press Association World Press Freedom, Islam and Human Rights.

ANDREW Cockburn, The United States is teaming up with Al Qaeda, again, Harper's, January 2016.

Antoni Abati Ninet, Modernity, Rationality and Constitutional Law in Muslim majority countries, The Danish Institute for Haman Rights, 2015.

Dale Ahlquist, G.K. Chesterton and the Use of the Imagination.

David L. Bergman and Glen C. Collins, The Law of Cause and Effect, Dominant Principle of Classical Physics,

(http://www.democracynow.org/03/2016)

Edward Gibbon and Simon Ocklay, History of the Saracen Empire, London, 1870.

Henry Phelps Brown, The Basis of Egalitarianism, Oxford, 1988.

Hunke, Sigrid. Le soleil d'Allah brille sur l'Occident, A. Michel (Espaces Libres), Paris,(1963), p.235-245.

141

Ian Millhiser, Understand Regime Change Better Than George W. Bush, Think Progress, 12/21/2015.

Janis Esots, Philosophical City, Encyclopedia of Islamic Political Thought, (PUP, 2012, ed. G. Bowering et al.) , Princeton.

Jean-Marie Guehenno, La fin de la democracie [the end of democracy], Flammarion, 1995.

Joe R. Feagin in "Agendas for the Twenty-First Century", University of Florida, February 2001.

John Foran, the climate change project.

JOHN RAWLS, A THEORY OF JUSTICE, the belknap press of Harvard University press Cambridge, Massachusetts, 1999.

Jose-Manuel Barreto , Human Rights and the Crisis of Modernity, Critical legal thinking, October 2009.

Karen Armstrong, Islam: A short History, The New York Times, 2002.

Nadia Yassine, Full Sails Ahead, JSP Publishing, 2006.

Nader Hashemi talks to Lewis Gropp, Islam, Sharia law and democracy, 03/2011.

Nicola Perugini, The Anthropologists at War,

The Universal Declaration of Human Rights.1948.

Peter Pels, The Anthropology of Colonialism, Amsterdam University, 1997.

Paul Johnson, Absolute evil Absolute Folly, Forbes, December 28, 2015.